The A-Z of Limericks

501 Personalized Rhymes

The A-Z of Limericks

501 Personalized Rhymes

by

Trevor P. Morley

Strategic Book Publishing and Rights Co.

Strategic Book Publishing and Rights Co.
12620 FM 1960, Suite A4-507
Houston TX 77065
www.sbpra.com

ISBN: 978-1-60976-074-8

Male A Names

When Archibald Met Liberace,
He Was Asked, "Do Our Wigs Look Too Starchy?"
He Replied, "Don't You Dare,
This Is My Real Hair,
So I'm Not Archibald, I'm Just Archie!"

When Andrew Went Off To The Coast,
His Girlfriend's Skin Started To Roast.
She Said, "Cream Me Up, Andy,
Not Smothered Or Sandy,"
But He Still Made Her Look Like A Ghost.

A Family Man Is Our Arthur,
He Is Known As A Real Belly Laugher,
With An Average Life,
And A Cuddly Wife,
And Two Point Four Kids, Not Two And Half, Yeah.

A Circus Man Named Alexander
Flies Trapeze While Inside Suits Of Armor,
Does It All With A Frown,
As He's Really A Clown,
To Punish The Pie-Facing Ringmaster.

Just Before His Vacation, Dear Alan
Went Off To A Small Tanning Salon.
His Friend Said, "Why Do This?
Before Holiday Bliss?"
Al Replied, "It's The Isle Of Man, Son!

A Right Cheeky* Monkey Named Arnold
Hangs Round His Mom's Neck With A Strong Hold.
Then He Climbs Down a Tree
With Style And Glee.
He's A Marmoset, Smallish And Bold.

* impudent

*Brash Albert's So Keen Spotting Birds,
That It's Quite Hard To Put Into Words.
He Takes Care Of Their Needs,
As The Wild Ones He Feeds,
And They Come Back For Seconds And Thirds.

* bold

Old Anthony, Tony, Or Ant,
Took A Ride On A Large Elephant,
Where He Tried A Trunk Call,
But His Ears Were Too Small,
He May Need A Drum/Trumpet Transplant.

With Abraham Linking His Chains,
He Made Anchors For Ships For His Pains.

He Was Once Dragged Aweigh,
Lost A Warship That Day,
And The Mystery How Still Remains.

A Courteous Person Is Adam,
How To Help, He Always Will Fathom.
If He Holds You The Door,
It's Through Friendship, For Sure.
If He's Clumsy, He'll Say, "Sorry, Madam."

A Perfect Light Snack For Aloysius
Is A Plate Full Of Line-Caught Fresh Fishes.
He Likes Fishin', Not Golfin'.
And Eats Like A Dolphin.
He'll Do Tricks Afterwards, If One Wishes.

Male B Names

On A Comfortable Mattress Lay Brian;
Its Clean Sheets Had Just Had An Iron.
Did He Know What He Said
As He Lay In The Bed?
Or, Perhaps, Some Sleep Talk He Was Tryin'.

The Clumsiness Shown By Young Barry
Is The Reason That He'll Never Marry.
He Feels So Ashamed,
Thinks He's Always Been Framed,
He's All Thumbs At The Town Cash And Carry.

* A type of store

Old Butch Is A Tough Guy At Heart,
And His Bellowing Voice Fits the Part,
But Not Just on His Own,
But Through A Large Megaphone—
This Seven-Stone Man Needs Head Start.

A Bonk On The Head Shook Poor Bert,
But For Once, Was A Fortunate Hurt,
He Said, "I Was Dense,

4

Now I've Plenty Of Sense,
If You Take Me On Now You'll Eat Dirt!"

Old Benjamin Calls Himself "Ben,"
He Will Use His Full Name Now And Then.
If He Writes A Report,
And Then Signs His Name Short,
It Would Lengthen The Life Of His Pen.

Builder Barney Got Into Real Trouble,
So His Manager Burst Barney's Bubble.
The Debris On The Site,
Caused By Working All Night,
Was A Pile Of Pure Barmy* Rubble.

* Crazy

On Brendan All Hopes Were Depending,
And It Could Have Been Just So Heart-Rending,
But The Pressure Did Stop
When He Hit Double Top*,
And His Pub Mates Had One Happy Ending.

* A dart game

Bernard Thinks He's A Bit Of A Saint,
But I'll Say This, Before We All Faint.
He Has Saved Men From Mountains
And Pulled Others From Fountains,
But The Saints Are All Dead, And He Ain't.

Bartholomew's Birthday Is Near,
He Wants Presents, That's Perfectly Clear,
And A Cake That's Enticing
With His Name Spelt In Icing,
His Full Name, Not "Bart"—Do You Hear?

A Happy Young Biker Named Bradley
Really Needed His Fringe Cutting Badly.
But Just As He Feared,
He Was Quite Over-Sheared,
So He Slinked From The Barber's Quite Sadly.

Basil Had Quite A Brush With The Law,
And Was Almost Pinned Down To The Floor.
But When Back At The Station,
He Said, With Elation,
"You Can't Book Me For Being A Bore!"

Male C Names

A Ballroom Instructor Named Charles
Is Attracted To All Of the Girls.
For The Ladies' Sweet Sakes,
He Gets Paid Off In Cakes,
So It's Waltzes For Viennese Whirls.

Old Christopher Acts Like a Saint,
So His Track Record Has Not A Taint,
Except For One Time,
After Drinking Some Lime,
When He Bleached The Priest, Making Him Faint.

The Semi-Pro Gardener, Colin,
Was Outside When The Rain Started Fallin',
So Inside He Did Go
And Abandoned His Hoe.
"Drink Time For My Blooms!" He Said, Bawlin'.

When Injured At Sports, Poor Young Clint
Went Walking Around In A Splint.
So He Had To Demur
And Said, "So Sorry, Sir,
But I Can't Do Today's Relay Sprint!"

When Claude Clawed His Way Up The Wall,
He Made Doubly Sure Not To Fall.
With His Pulleys And Rope,
And A Line To The Pope,
He Had Power To Rise Above All.

Cedric Used To Work Out On A Farm
Until Losing The Use Of An Arm.
People Said, "That Old Fool,
Was He Milking A Bull?"
He Got Gored, Causing Quite An Alarm.

So Offended Indeed, Felt Our Craig,
That He Took His Appeal To The Hague.
He Wanted Full Compensation
From a Radio Station,
But Their Libelous Words Were Too Vague.

Chesney Loves Hawks, Owls, And Eagles,
And He Also Likes Bassets And Beagles.
He Enjoys Most Wildlife,
And So, Too, Does His Wife,
Except Perhaps, Pigeons And Seagulls!

The Best Soccer Goal Scored By Cyril
Was In Austria's Mountainous Tirol.
His Strike From Halfway

Made The Spectators' Day,
Burst The Net, And Showed Off His Hill Skill.

Clifford Felt Stiff As A Board,
So He Pulled The Emergency Cord.
When He Shot From The Plane,
He Thought He Was Flying Again,
But Fell Into The Emergency Ward!

A Famous Old Mime, Known As Calvin,
Would Never Have Uttered A Foul Thing,
Until A Fully Blind Group
Came And Joined Him For Soup,
They Could Not Hear A Word He Was Mouthing.

Male D Names

Old David's A Whiz With A Lathe,
But One Morning It Wouldn't Behave.
So He Lost All His Knack,
And Thought He'd Get Fired/Sack.
And He Did Anyway. Sorry, Dave!

A Northerly Outing For Derek
Took Him Off To The Fair Town Of Berwick.
The One Thing He'd Need,
Was Some Clothing Of Tweed,
So He Might Cross The Border To Get It.

When Daniel Has Time On His Hands,
He Goes Off And Watches Brass Bands.
The Tubas And Horns
Always Light Up His Morns,
Afternoon, Evening, Night, Egg-Time Sands.

The Big Day Arrived For Old Darren;
On The Motorway, Sounding His Car Horn,
He's A Liverpool Fan,
With A 3 p.m. Plan,
With The Queen, He's A Lord, The Red Baron!

Our Donald's The Neatest Of Men,
And He Won't Leave The Top Off His Pen.
He Has Exquisite Taste,
Not A Cushion's Misplaced,
So I Give Him A Nine Out Of Ten.

The Dustbin Was Dusted By Dustin,
Which Had Always Been Full, Almost Bustin'.
He Cleaned It With Swipes,
Using Lemony Wipes,
As He Thought This Would Stop It From Rustin'.

The Technical Genius Of Damon
May Just Mesmerize Many A Layman,
But His Lectures Do Bore,
Numbing Folks To The Core,
If The Crowd Fell Asleep, Could You Blame Them?

Well Dressed, To Work Early Came Dean,
So His Boss Said, "My, My, You Are Keen."
Was He Up At First Light?
Or Did He Stay Up All Night?
The Latter! He Looked A Bit Green.

I Wouldn't Call Dennis A Menace,
Though He Does Tend To Cheat, Playing Tennis.
When He Hammers The Ball

He Always Argues The Call,
And I'm Not The First Person To Pen This!

With Our Dominic In A Republic,
He Checked Out A Night Club, Real Quick.
But It Wasn't To His Taste—
Beer Like Wallpaper Paste—
So, He Left The Republic, Quite Sick.

The Speech Just Provided By Duncan
Turned Out To Be Absolute Bunkum.
Though People Paid Him Good Money
Just To Hear Something Funny,
His Ridiculous Rants Really Sunk 'Em.

Male E Names

Although Eric Has Never Been Rich,
Had A MasterCard, Visa, Or Switch,
He Does Have A Pot
Near His Cabbage Patch Plot,
At The Rainbow's End, Wedged In A Ditch.

When Ernest Went Down On One Knee
To Propose To His Good Wife-To-Be,
She Said, "You're So Sweet,
The Best Bloke I Could Meet,
But I'll Need Three Divorces, First, Ernie!"

An Equestrian Rider Named Ewan
Flew To Try A Gymkhana In Turin.
He Flew Out Again Fast,
After Finishing Last,
And He Thought His Horse Needed Re-Shoein'.

On A Short Trip To Paris For Ellery,
He Got Pelted With Onions And Celery.
In The Notre Dame Stocks,
His Hunched Back Broke The Locks,
And Split The Whole Thing To Bits, Verily.

A Carpenter-Royal Named Edward
Makes Palatial Furniture Dead Good.
He Gets Plenty Of Practice
With Matchsticks In His Mattress,
Which Come Out When He Cannot Find Redwood.

When Elton Went Off To The John,
He Told Friends That He Wouldn't Be Long,
But While He Sat On The Bowl,
He Slipped Down The Hole,
And Was Fished From The Sea Of Hong Kong.

Old Elvis Got Slightly Shook Up
By A Hound Dog, When It Was A Pup.
The Only Pet He Wants To Share
Is A Cute Teddy Bear,
Which Once Won Him The Jailhouse Cup.

The Obvious Jibe About Eustace
Is, Of Course, "He Is Totally Useless."
Though This May Seem Unfair
To The People Who Care,
He's Got Brains, But If Not Used, He'll Lose This.

Immaculate Emmanuel, As We Could All Tell,
Was Looking So Smart, And So Well.
But In Church For A Wedding,

All His Skin Started Shedding.
That Snake Slithered In Time With The Bell.

An Adventurer Named Ebenezer
Is A Curious Kind Of Old Geezer.
He Has Trekked Pole To Pole,
Conquered Many A Goal,
But Still Can't Pry The Food From His Freezer!

Old Ed Was The Star Of A Show
On TV; It Was Not Long Ago.
When An Ad Should Appear,
He'd Recite From Shakespeare,
But Was Always Stopped In Mid-Flow.

Male F Names

Poor Old Francis, Who Worked In A Bank,
Had An Office That Certainly Stank.
He Said When He Quit,
"Well, Goodbye To This Pit.
I Won't Miss It At All, To Be Frank!"

A DNA Expert Named Felix
Was A Scotsman, With One Or Two Wee Tricks.
He Spoke, Calm And Astute,
At The Women's Institute,
And Then Showed Them His Large Double Helix.

Frederick, Fred, Or Maybe It's Freddie,
Was Rather Attached To His Teddy.
His Mum Said, "Son, No More,
You're Now Aged Thirty-Four,
Give It Up!" ."No," He Said, "Still Not Ready."

While USA Flying Was Finn,
He Got Into A Turbulence Spin.
After Landing On End,
He Phoned An Old Friend,
To Tell Them The State He Was In.

The Trouble With Old Farmer Faron
Is That Half Of His Land Is Now Barren.
So He's Selling Up Soon,
Yes, Indeed, End Of June,
But He's Keeping His Large Rabbit Warren.

When Ferdinand Met The Archduke,
He Thought It Was Some Kind Of Fluke.
This Liverpool Boy
Was So Filled Full Of Joy,
He Didn't Know He'd Be Signing His Book.

The Destructive-Behaving Fitzroy
Laughs At Every Blown-To-Bits Toy.
When He Plays Battleships,
And Enough Squares He's Hits,
A Quick Salvo Could Bring Him Blitz Joy.

A Job Center Assistant Named Floyd
Spent His Days With The Mass Unemployed,
Till He Lost This Fine Job,
When He Dressed Like A Slob,
But His Life Guard Training Left Him Buoyed.

The Last Parachute Jump Made By Ford
Left Him Feeling As Stiff As A Board.
It Was One Low Jump Practice,

But He Just Couldn't Hack This,
Or Find The Emergency Cord!

A Professional Jockey Named Fabian
Likes His Horses To All Be Arabian.
They're Quite Used To The Dust,
So Dry Ground Is A Must,
Did He Win On The Soft. Really None.

An Accident-Prone Cop Named Fraser
Shot Himself In The Leg With A Taser,
Thought He Had Hold Of Truncheon,
Till He Heard A Slight Crunchin',
All Those Volts Were A Real Hair-Raiser!

Male G Names

A Lucky Goalkeeper Is Gary;
When A Penalty Kick He Did Parry,
Its Deflection Went Far,
Hit Both Posts And The Bar,
But Across The Goal-Line Did Not Carry.

A Notable Artist Named George
Runs A Business Quite Near Cheddar Gorge,
Sells Van Goghs And Rembrandts,
Da Vincis For Finance;
Each One He Will Expertly Forge.

Graham Does All His Shopping Online,
Even When The Day's Weather Is Fine.
He Gets Milk, Ham, And Eggs,
'Cause He's Saving His Legs
For A Trip To The Cellar, With Wine.

Since Gabriel Made The School Team,
The Colors He Wears Are A Dream.
Then He Stops And He Thinks,
"This Is Just Tiddlywinks!"
And He Lets Out A Laugh And A Scream.

A Jovial Person Named Gordon
Spends His Time As A Street Traffic Warden.
But One Day, With A Sob,
"Said, I Don't Like This Job,
As I Hate To Upset A Car Moron."

A Genealogy Expert Named Grant
Tracked Down His Once-Favorite Aunt.
When He Stopped Round For Tea,
He Climbed Family Tree,
Even Though She Had Said That He Can't.

He Has Fallen On Hard Times, Has Gregory,
And Is Now In Extreme State Of Beggary.
Though A Hospital Stay,
Kept Him Dry For A Day,
He Was Pleased, As He Got His False Leg Free!

Geoff Announced All The Soccer Match Scores,
Said Who Scored The Goals, And Who For.
The Crowd Roared, "Louder, Geoff,
We're A Little Bit Deaf."
It's The Faulty P.A., Not His Jaw!

As Gareth's A Lover Of Steam,
He Is Proud Of His Locos That Gleam,
And His Engines Of Traction
Give Him Great Satisfaction.
He's Just Thrilled To Be Part Of The Team.

A Knight Of The Garter, Named Gerald

Has Some News That He Wishes To Herald.

"They'll Be Jousting Tonight,

Two Bald Men Want To Fight,

But Don't Crave Too Much Action, Since They're Old!"

With Gavin Asleep In His Bed,

His Dog Brought Him A Postcard, Which Read,

"It's Your Boss, GET UP NOW!"

Doggy Woke Him Somehow,

The Alarm Clock Then Fell On Gav's Head.

Male H Names

When Harvey Kissed England Goodbye,
He Went Not By Sea Or By Sky.
Wouldn't Let Truck Or Train,
Car Or Van, Take The Strain,
But A Chunnel* Cart Horse. Don't Know Why!

* The tunnel under the English Channel, between England and France

Too Few New Small-Screen Stars Knew Hugh,
But He Wanted To Say, "How D'you Do?"
Then His Best Friend, One Day,
Came And Whisked Him Away,
Into Studio Two, "Doctor Who!"*

* A British sci-fi show

Henry Wanted Some Fun On The Beach,
Where Two Frisbees Were Thrown. He Missed Each.
Then He Shouted To Land,
"Help! I'm Stuck In Quicksand.
Can You Pass Me A Snorkel And Reach?"

One Thing You Can Never Call Howard
Is A Sniveling, Gibbering, Coward.

Though He Does Enjoy Custard,
And Cutting The Mustard,
And He Doesn't Mind Cream When It's Soured.

A Big Movie Buff, Known As Hector,
Bought Himself A Big-Screen Film Projector.
When The Tape It Did Snap,
He Said, "That's A Wrap,"
And He Had To Call Out The Inspector.

An Army Lance Corporal, Harrison,
Was Taking Some Leave In The Paris Sun,
But He Hated His Meals,
Garlic, Onions And Snails,
So He Thought He'd Go Back To His Garrison.

An Alcohol Drinker Named Harold
Bought A Measure Of Rum, Which Was Barreled.
It'd Been Out In The Sun
Since June, 1901,
Though You'd Never Believe It Was That Old!

After Eating His Haggis, Young Hamish,
Asked Of His Sister A Lame Wish:
"Do My Homework For Me,
And You'll Have Cake And Tea."
When Refused, Hamish Said, "Not To Blame, Miss."

A Champion Angler Named Herbert
Thought He'd Landed The World's Largest Turbot.
But It Was A Blue Whale,
Sank The Boat He Did Sail,
And All That On A Line Laced With Sherbet!

A Rugby Official Named Homer
Is Renowned As A Bit Of A Roamer.
He's All Over The Pitch*,
Though He Has One Small Glitch,
He Floods It, 'Cause He's A Mouth Foamer!

* Field

When Hank Pulled A Prank At The Bank,
Its Security Made His Heart Dank.
He Then Said, "I'm No Tool,
It's Just My April Fool.
I Have Plenty More Left In The Tank!"

Male I Names

A Shady Young Person Named Ian,
From Police Was Quite Hurriedly Fleeing,
On A Golf Course Did Hide,
But Took A Blow To His Pride,
After Putting A Man Off His Teeing.

A Fairground Magician Named Ivor
Used His Assistant's Perfume To Revive Her.
She'd Been Just Sawed In Half,
Made The Paying Folk Laugh,
Wasn't Glued Back Right Way 'Round, Either!

When Isaac Signed Up With A Gym,
It Was Not Off The Cuff, On A Whim,
But Because Of A Row,
With His Former Best Pal,
And Right Now, He Could Pulverize Him.

"Indiana Wants Me,"* He Heard Said.
"I Do Not," He Replied, "You're Misled."
He'd Lost All His Patience
For Nostalgic Song Stations,
Tried The Voice Of America, Instead.

* A 1970 hit song by R. Dean Taylor

When Ivan Took Dives From A Height,
Things Didn't Look Terribly Right.
And The Replays Suggest,
The Dive Wasn't His Best,
As His Trunks Were Two Sizes Too Tight.

A CIA Agent Named Ira
Was All Fitted Up With A Wire, Yeah.
When His Mission Did Fail,
Got Disguised With A Veil,
But His Boss Said, "I've Still Gotta Fire Ya."

A Silent Horror Flick Actor Named Igor
Made The Crummiest Movie That We Saw.
It Was Meant To Have Sound,
But With Camera Cables Swapped 'Round,
It Did Not Show The Colors He Wore!

A Cruel Theatre Critic Named Inigo
Found Himself One Day In A Show.
"Greased Lightning!" He Said,
Then He Woke Up In Bed.
Now He Won't Be So Harsh With His Pen, You Know?

A Fine Waiter Of Tables Is Irving.
He Loves Chatting To Guests He Is Serving.
But His Eye Corner Saw

Someone Pea-d On The Floor

He Grasped The Veg While His Free Hand Was Swerving!

A NASA Space Scientist, Irwin

Had Been Wondering What Was Occurring.

The Dark Side Of The Moon?

No, The Top Of His Spoon;

Wondered Why Telescopes Had Been Whirring.

A Juggernaut Driver Named Ishmael

Was Once Asked If He'd Ever Gone Fishtail.

He Said, "When I Was Young,"

And Then Stuck Out His Tongue,

Then He Forked It, He Does Like To Kiss/Tell.

Male J Names

When Businessman John Had Time Free,
He Went Out On A Large Shopping Spree.
While Enjoying His Day,
With His Wife Out Of The Way,
He Did Say, "She Spends Far More Than Me!"

When Joel Took His Role On The Dole*,
He Said, "My New Goal Is To Bowl.
I'm So Good At Cricket,
That I Might Take A Wicket.
If I Miss A Hill Whole, Made By Mole."

* Welfare

When Jeffrey Arrived At His Work,
He At Once Looked A Bit Of A Berk*.
His Lower Clothing Fell Down,
As He'd Lost Seven Pounds,
Hadn't Cashed In His Fruity Cake Perk.

* Fool

When Jonathan's Out And About,
He Often Goes Fishing For Trout.

By Bank Or By Boat,
He'll Be Clearing His Throat,
And When He Lands A Fish, Shouts, "There's No Doubt!"

A Master Of All Trades Is Jack,
And He Really Does Put Up Your Back,
With So Many Jobs On,
Problem-Free All Day Long,
We Would Laugh If He Got Fired Or Sacked.

A Top Fire-Eater Is James,
And He Does This While Juggling Frames.
Then He Leaves With His Daughter,
For Some Strong Firewater,
He Needs Something To Put Out The Flames.

A Soccer Supporter Named Julian
Could Never Be Classed As A Hooligan.
He Missed A Goal Yesterday
As He Was Knitting Away,
Making Booties For One Player's New Son!

An Example To Many Is Joshua,
Well Turned Out, With A Wardrobe Of Posh New Gear.
A Consultant Of Style,
With A Twinkling Smile,
You Can Hire, If You Have Enough Dosh, Oh Yeah!

The Finest Minesweeper, Named Joseph,
Has No Fear When He Finds An Explosive.
His Drills Gave Joe The Skill,
To Turn Bomb Threats To Nil;
No One Knows When There's More, No One Knows If.

Very Long Fingernails Had Jeremy;
He Trimmed Them With A Thin Board Of Emery.
For A Bet And A Laugh,
Grew Them A Year And A Half.
Now When Scratching, They're A Less Painful Memory.

Chef Jake Tried His Greatest Cake Bake,
But Then Said, "Heaven's Sake, What's It Take?"
He Got Covered In Pastry,
And Said, "Well, That's No So Tasty,"
Bounced A Piece Round The Room—Didn't Break.

Male K Names

A Motorbike Rider Named Kevin
Annoyed Neighbors With Far Too Much Revvin'.
But In Time, Changed His Ways
From His Hell's Angels' Phase.
His New Moped Sounds Like Pure Heaven.

Kenneth's Really The Star Of The Show,
Stage and Screen, Online, Radio.
But He Once Blew A Fuse
Reporting Local News,
Saying, "I'm A Great Actor, You Know?"

The Thief Of Keith's Teeth And His Beef
Had Police Out All Night In Welsh Neath,
But They Just Simply Saw
A Man Holding His Jaw,
And Some Gristle. It's Beyond Belief!

A Meddlesome Person Is Kieran,
As He Just Cannot Stop Interferin'.
When He Sticks In His Oar*,
His Friends Show Him The Door,
And They Ban Him From Back-Seat Car Steerin'.

* Meddles

31

A Student Of Law, Known As Kelvin,
Said His Course's Last Year He Was Shelvin'.
When His Mum Asked, "What For?"
"Makes Me Cry, No Rapport,"
He Replied. From His Heart He Was Delvin'.

When Kyle Spent A While On The Nile,
He Said, "Think I'll Rile That Old Crocodile."
Didn't Do What He Oughta,
Pulled A Face In Fresh Water,
And The Croc Bit Him Right On The Dial*.

* British slang for "face"

Old Kane, Who's Got Grain For a Brain,
Felt The Strain, Once Again, On His Crane.
The Street Flooded With Water,
Nearly Drowning His Daughter,
Missed The Gas, But Snapped A Large Aqua Main!

Keanu Revealed More Than He Should
When He Wandered Off Into The Wood.
Not A Dirty Old Man,
But A Spy For Japan,
He Made All The Bears Grizzle*He Could!

* Complain

Just How Apathetic Is Kirk?
Well, He's Certainly Not Keen On His Work.

But He's Now A Sperm Donor
For The Feminine Loner,
His Child Support He Does Shirk!

The Portrayal Of Past Battles For Kurt,
Often Sees Him End Up In The Dirt.
If He Jousts On A Horse,
And Falls Off With Some Force,
He Just Says, "Well, I'm Not Really Hurt."

Karl Knows Just How Many Bets Work,
And Can Throw Double Six With A Jerk.
Probability And Chance
He Computes With A Glance,
But He Won't Tell The Casino His Perk*.

* Advantage

Male L Names

When Laurence Hopped Onto His Speedboat,
Which Was Nicely Afloat On His Fort Moat,
It Went At Quite A Low Speed,
In Fact, No Speed, Indeed;
The Keys Were At Home, In His Coat.

At A Ballroom Dance Trial, Poor Lionel
Thought For A While He'd Make Final,
But Then In The Last Dance,
He Got Locked In A Stance,
In His Over-Starched Shirt—His Wife Irons Them All.

"It's Good To Be Free!" Shouted Lee,
"My Plea Brought To Me Clemency."
Then He Said, With A Wail,
"Now My Wedding I Won't Fail,
If I Don't Get Tied Back To That Tree!"

Leonard's A Top Writer Of Books,
And The Type He Writes Often Has Hooks;
Fishing, DIY, Sewing,
Is The Stuff That He's Knowing;
You Can Tell All His Tomes By Their Looks.

A Poor Lanky Student Is Lance,
Earns Some Cash By Tending To Plants.
He's Called "Beanpole" Or "Weed"
When His Friends Feel The Need,
But He'll Think Of Them When He's In France.

Leslie Fancies The Turn Of A Card,
And To Read This Man Is Quite Hard.
But One Night During Poker,
He Captured A Joker,
And He Laughed, As Its Features Were Scarred.

A Street-Circus Performer Named Lester
Felt His Act Was Beginning To Fester,
Did The Same Thing Each Day,
For A Pittance Of Pay,
Until Starting His Job As Court Jester!

Lennox Threw His White Ball To The Ground,
As He Played Out A Beach Golfing Round.
Wanted Out, Couldn't Win,
But Played On; Tide Came In,
Lost A Round, Ball Not Found, Nearly Drowned.

Lewis Just Won The Ham-Eating Crown;
You'd Not Think So, On Seeing His Frown.
But This Meat-Eating Freak

Has A Long Winning Streak.
Bacon Too, The Rashest Guy In Town!

He Thought He Had Blue Blood, Did Luke,
That Is Why All His Friends Called Him "Duke."
But On Bashing His Head,
Gushing Fluid Was Red,
And He Murmured, "Well, That Was A Fluke."

On A Long Desert Journey, Old Lincoln
Was In Desperate Need Of Some Drinkin'.
Thought He Saw A Mirage,
But It Was A Garage,
So He Walked Right Past. What Was He Thinkin'?

Male M Names

Such A Low Carbon Footprint Has Michael,
As He Goes Everywhere On A Cycle,
Though He Did Steal A Wheel,
When He Lost a Circus Deal,
And His Uni Became Bi At The Trike Stall*.

* Store

When Mark Took A Stroll In The Park,
His Bull Mastiff Was Having A Lark.
When They Reached An Oak Tree,
A Girl Said, "Your Dog Has Bit Me!"
He Said, "Sorry, Bite's Worse Than His Bark!"

Mitchell Has Got Several Brothers,
Who Each Have Significant Others,
But Has No One Himself,
And Is Left On The Shelf,
So It's Just Mitchell's Brothers With Lovers.

A Bit Of A Hoarder Is Martin,
With His Junk, He Just Cannot Bear Partin',
Or Perhaps It's Too Far,

As He's Not Got A Car
For Trips To The Dump—Too Much Cartin'.

He Loves Ablutions, Does Malcolm;
A Hot Bath Is, Indeed, Very Welcome.
He Spends Many Hours
'Mongst The Fragrance Of Flowers,
Then He Covers His Rear End In Talcum.

Manfred's The Man For The Job,
If Your Garden Is Making You Sob.
He Once Grew Every Dahlia
In Western Australia,
And Sold Them For Quite A Few Bob.

A Home Carpentry Fitter Named Melvin
Needs Some Help When He's Putting Up Shelvin'.
His Level's Unsound,
He'll Need More Than A Pound,
To Replace Them, In His Wallet He's Delvin'!

Maxwell's House Was So Full Up With Junk,
And Waste Rotting, It Smelled Like A Skunk.
His Family Did A House Clearance,
And Max Gave No Interference,
They Untied Him, Then Played Some Kerplunk!

Marlon's Bran Does Get Ate In The Morning,
He Says, Could Prevent Him From Snoring.
With His Head Dipped In A Bowl,
And Flakes Stuck To His Nose Hole,
He Would Sleep On His Back Until Dawning.

A Religiously Handy Man, Matthew,
Was Repairing A Flat Pew With That Glue,
But It Wasn't Quite Set;
Someone Got Stuck, I Bet,
And The Parson Said, "I Will Not Thank You!"

A Sensitive Issue For Miles
Means He's No Longer Wall-To-Wall Smiles.
He Prefers Now To Stand,
In The Air, Sea, Or Land.
It's A Quite Nasty Thing, Called Piles!**

** Hemorrhoids

Male N Names

When Nicholas Got Covered In Paint,
Red And White, Though A Little Bit Faint,
This Round Man Still Laughed So,
With A Big Ho, Ho, Ho.
He's So Giving, The Mark Of A Saint.

A Big Beefy Person Is Norman;
That's Why He Works Nights As A Doorman.
Though He Has A Limp Wrist,
It's Attached To A Fist
That Looks Like A Boxer's, Named Foreman.

As Nigel Was Making His Plans
To Join The Military, Black And Tans*,
His Mates Helped Him, Not Very,
Pick A Khaki Suit And Black Beret.
He Was Issued Them, Along With The Armbands.

* An army unit

An Arctic Explorer Named Neil
Doesn't Quite Have True Nerves Of Steel.

He Was Dealt A Low Blow,
Stubbed His Toe On The Snow,
Crippled, Hasn't Left London. Unreal!

Nelson's Not A Good Agony Uncle,
And He Works For A Big News Carbuncle.
Its Writers Grow Solemn
When They View Nelson's Column.
He Gives Readers Bad News. Hopes! He's Sunk All!

Nathan Does Like To Go For A Swim,
Have A Jog, Ride A Bike, Go To Gym.
But As Fit As He Is,
He's No Good At A Quiz.
Brain Agility? Simply Not Him.

The Unusual Actions Of Neville
Make You Think He's Not Quite On The Level.
I Mean, Who Slurps His Soup
While He's Looping The Loop?
Is He Training To Be A Bread Devil?

While Norris Was Blackening Shoes,
He Forgot About Cold Winter Blues.
But He Sleepwalked One Night,
And His Boots Went Snow White.
They're The Only Ones, Now, That He Will Use.

He's A Tidy Park Angel, Is Noah,
But His Working Suit Makes Him Go Slower,
Placing Rubbish In Sacks,
Wrapper, Tin, Box, Or Packs,
His Two-At-Once Method's A Goer!

Napoleon's Dynamite Treats
Leave His Fans All Transfixed In Their Seats.
His Jokes Get A Huge Laugh,
But That's Only The Half,
Chairs Are Glued, Fans Can't Get To Their Feet!

A Soccer Skills Striker Named Noel
Had The Ball At His Feet, By The Goal.
He Cocked His Foot In The Box,
Fell To Ground; Tangled Socks,
Missed The Chance, Now He Lives On The Dole!*

* Welfare

Male O Names

Oliver, The Double-Act Straight Man,
Filmed A Scene Right Beside An Ice Cream Van.
Holding A Cornet Was Folly,
His Partner Said, "Gee, Sorry, Ollie."
His Clumsy Trip Really Looked Rather Deadpan.

Owen's Cash Flowing Is Slowing,
Since He's No Longer Going To Rowing.
He'd A Sponsorship Deal,
His Gold Medal Was Real,
But He Lost Both. There's No Cash, And No Knowing!

So Engrossed With The Performance Was Oscar,
As He Sat Through A Showing Of Tosca.
It Took Someone From Higher,
To Put Out His Wig Fire,
From The Accident Stoppage Group, RoSPA*.

* Royal Society for the Prevention of Accidents

At An English Exam Sat Young Ozzy,
Saying "Should I Write, 'Were He', Or 'Was He'?"
Then He Said, With A Blow,

"I'm Not Shakespeare, You Know?
My Brain's Gone. I Got Bit By A Mozzy.*"

* Mosquito

Orlando's A Blooming Good Man,
And He's Got Such A Lovely Tan.
Did He Get It From Florida?
No, Just Down The Corridor,
The Treatment Room, England's Luton Town.

Not Appearing Too Brainy Was Omar;
Teachers Said That He Probably Won't Go Far.
But He Found Things To Sell,
Like A Large Oil Well,
And A Patented New Brand Of Foamer.

With Olaf Now Losing His Hair,
At The Wig And Toupee Fair, He's There.
But They Said, "The Wrong Size,"
As They Covered His Eyes,
And He Looked Like A Brown Grizzly Bear!

An Ice Skating Novice Named Orville
Thought One Day That He'd Match Dean And Torvill.
On A Wire He'd Fly,
Like His Namesake, In The Sky,
Not The Duck, The Wright Brother! He Sure Will.

Otis Traveled To Berkshire Reading,
But All He Came Back With, Was Bedding.
He Got Trapped In A Quilt,
Then Rolled Home, With A Tilt,
It's The Form Of Transport He Was Dreading!

Orson Wells Up In Tears His Blue Eyes,
When He Sees Anybody Who Cries,
And He Feels Sympathetic,
For People Athletic,
Sobbing When They Win Medals, No Lies.

His Lifestyle Has Changed Now For Otto,
Since He Won On The National Lotto.
He Can Now Buy Two Lines,
For Five Weeks, Happy Signs,
As He Won't Spend The Cash Getting Blotto!

Male P Names

When Paul Scaled A Wall That Was Tall,
His Fall Didn't Gall Him At All.
Though His Training Was Tough,
He Is Made Of Stern Stuff,
And Can Header* A Medicine Ball.

* Propel a ball with his head, as in soccer

Left Back On The Sidelines Is Patrick,
Even Though He Last Week Scored A Hat Trick.
Didn't Change His Position
At The Game's Intermission,
Scored Three Own-Goals*, His Defense Was So Static.

* Own goal: a goal accidentally scored against your own team

As Philip Took Off In His Plane,
He Said, "Looks A Little Like Rain."
He Thought His Craft Was Of Paper,
And Was Revived With Some Vapor,
Saying, "Oh, Was I Dreaming Again?"

A Calligraphy Expert Is Peter,
And His Writing Is Very Much Neater

Than All Of His Friends'
In The Letters He Sends,
Including Those Using Computer.

A Wine-From-Pears Drinker Is Perry;
It's Been Known To Make Him A Tad Merry.
Did I Say Just "A Tad"?
It Depends What He's Had,
So Sometimes You May Have To Say "Very!"

Percy's A Green-Fingered Chap,
And He's Draining His Tree Of Its Sap.
He Says, "May I Have Another,
For I Wish To Make Rubber,
And Some Glue For My Tape, That's A Wrap."

A Pro Document Signer Named Parker
Lost His Pen, So He Used A Black Marker.
His Writing Was Thick,
Like A Small Oil Slick,
With The Letters Incredibly Darker.

A Wedding Cake Baker Named Piers
Was One Day The Main Subject Of Jeers.
On A Couple's Big Day,
The Icing Melted Away;
The Bride Knew It Would All End In Tiers.

An Old DVD Lover Named Preston
Sat Down To Enjoy A Nice Western,
Eating Sweets, Drinking Pop,
Paused The Flick, For A Stop,
As He Gave Himself Mild Indigestion.

Pascal Likes To Program Computers;
He's Self Taught, He Doesn't Need Tutors.
If It's Business Or Pleasure,
He's A Real Software Treasure,
And He Foils Any Internet Looters.

If I Told You The Story Of Prince,
There's A Chance That It Might Make You Wince.
Clumsy Person Is He,
Door Slammed Finger, Grazed Knee,
Injured Childhood, And Many Days Since.

Male Q Names

A Motoring Guru Named Quentin
Had A Fault With The Car He Was Rentin'.
Then A Man Cried, "Oh, No!
That's A Car Just For Show.
It's The Prototype I'm Still Inventin'!"

So Small And So Mighty Is Quinn,
That Most Sizes Of Tub He'll Fit In.
He's As Strong As An Ox,
Can Punch Through A Cardboard Box,
Though Perhaps Not A Large Baked Bean Tin.

Quinton's Got Stripes On The Brain,
Though His Shirts Always Start Off So Plain.
Had He Just Been Run Over
By A Mower, In Clover?
Or Was The Park Bench Just Painted Again?

Keeps Up With The Joneses Does Quincy,
His Competitiveness Makes You Wince, See.
Above Everything Else
He Can Even Speak Welsh,
Not A Lot, Boyo, Here, Just A Teensy.

Cleaning Clothes Is A Real Chore For Quintin,
And The Worst Part Is When He's De-Lintin'.
For One Day By Surprise,
The Fluff Stuck To His Eyes,
And Damaged His Contact Lens Tintin'.

Quintus Is The Fifth Blued-Eyed Boy
In A Family Filled Full With Joy.
Mum And Dad Think He's Great,
But Had Six, Seven, Eight,
And They All Had To Share The Same Toy!

Male R Names

A Rugby Club Groundsman Named Richard
Endeavors To Not Make The Pitch* Hard.
When Game Time Does Expire,
It's Become A Quagmire,
Those Size Eighteen Boots Are Now Ditch-Tarred.

* Field

In A Farm Field, Young Robert Was Tilling,
Before Digging Up Crops, And Some Milling.
"It's Harrowing," He Said,
With A Marrow On His Head,
Though It's Not Quite The Beans He Was Spilling.

A Bit Of A Baby Is Ryan;
I've Lost Count Of The Tears He's Been Cryin'.
"Grow Up!" Said His Mom,
"And Stop Sucking Your Thumb."
He Replied, "Ma, I'm Three, And I'm Tryin!"

Reginald Had A Fall And A Rise,
Before Taking His Wife By Surprise.
He Said, "Please Call Me Reggie,

Don't Eat Meat, I'm A Veggie,
And From Now On I'll Wear A Disguise!"

Everybody Loves Raymond, You Know,
He's Not Just Some Old So-And-So,
With A Heart Made Of Gold,
And The Chivalry Of Old,
He's A Ray Of Sun Melting The Snow.

A Kilt Of Newspaper Wore Russell,
While Engaged In A Big Courtroom Tussle.
When He Gave The Judge Some Lip,
He Was Torn Off A Strip.
It Was Lucky He'd Donned A Ladies' Bustle!*

* An undergarment worn in the 1800s

So Clumsy At Snooker Was Rupert,
He Once Wondered Just Where Was His Cue Put.
It Had Dropped Down His Clothes,
From His Head To His Toes,
Celebrated A Pot? Needs A New Shirt.

An Origami Grand Master Named Ronald
Ran An Arts And Crafts Shop So Bright And Bold.
But It Ran Out Of Cash,
And The Poor Place Did Crash,
It Unfortunately Really Did Fold.

A Man Of High Office, Named Robin
Spends Most Of His Work Days Hobnobbin',
Though On Sundays, It Seems,
He Prefers Custard Creams,
Or A Bourbon In His Mouth He'll Be Lobbin'.

A Freelance Rat Catcher Named Roland
Was Once On Assignment In Poland.
We All Saw His Success,
Via TV And Press;
His Blog Had The Most Hits In The Whole Land.

A Shortsighted Builder Named Rex
Was Once Told That He Needed Some Specs.
He Once Built A Whole House,
Which Would Just Fit A Mouse;
He Builds Homes Now, Big, Strong, And They Flex.

Male S Names

Angler Stephen, Or Could It Be Steve,
Saw A Genie Slip Out Of His Sleeve.
So He Asked For One Wish,
"Stop Me Smelling Of Fish!"
It Was Something He Could Not Achieve.

An Experienced Motorist Is Samuel,
Learning All That He Can From A Manual.
Driving Car, Bus Or Van,
Heavy Goods, Tractor, Man,
His Insurance Is Large And Paid Annual.

This Simplest Message To Simon
Is To Not Use Two Words That Aren't Rhymin'!
The Ones That He'll Choose
Should Just Fit Like A Noose,
Otherwise It's A Face Full Of Pie, Man!

His Name, Stuart Can Shorten To Stu,
By The Masses, Or Maybe The Few.
But Which Does He Prefer?
The Full Length Or Shorter?
You Could Ask, Guess, Or Maybe You Knew.

A Marathon Runner Named Silas
Plays "Chariots Of Fire" With His Stylus.
It's On Vinyl, Of Course,
And He Runs Like A Horse,
On His Treadmill, Which, Indeed, Is So Stylish.

An Englishman Well Known As Scott
Loved The Welsh Dragon Spray On His Pot.
His Irish Parents Were Fair,
But, For Him, Felt Despair,
Till He Won U.S. Idol! Great Shot!

A Novice Farm Worker Named Sean
Was Preparing A Field For Its Corn.
But The Farmer Said, "No!
That Is Not Where You Go.
You've Just Plowed Up My Lovely Front Lawn!"

A Cross-Country Runner Named Shane
Was Beginning To Feel The Race Strain.
Looking At The Home Straight,
He Was Dealt A Cruel Fate,
Being Told He Must Go 'Round Again.

A Man From The Tropics, Named Seth,
Doesn't Speak His, "T-H," As An "F."
He Says "Please" And "Tanks,"

Though "Tinks" He Sometimes Blanks,
As He's Also A Little Bit Deaf.

A Big Soccer Striker Named Solomon
Can Beat Any Man He Sets Eyes Upon.
But He Got Cocky, Sol,
When He Missed An Open Goal,
Then Hit The Sand Pit With His Follow-On*.

* Next shot

Male T Names

A Nasty Thing Happened To Thomas
While Preparing A Large Plate Of Hummus.
His Window Got Smashed,
During Scotch Pair's Stramash;*
He'll Return Fire With Chick Peas, I Promise.

* During Scotch Pair's Stramash: During a disturbance at a golf or
  lawn bowling match

When Terence Was Brushing His Suit,
He Found In A Pocket Some Loot.
"It's Good Money!" Said Terry,
So He Put On His Beret,
And Then Went Out And Spent It On Fruit.

On A Crash Course Of Writing Was Trevor,
Though He Seemed To Make Quite Heavy Weather
Of The Homework He'd Got,
On A Puppy Named Spot,
There's No Start, Middle, End, Whatsoever.

Timothy's Always Minding His Language,
Though One Day, After Eating A Sandwich,

He Said, " Dash" And "Blow"
And Was Sent Down Below,
And Was Sorry For Causing Much Anguish.

They Say, "You're A Hair God" To Tyler;
People Think He's The World's Greatest Styler.
His Charge Is A Snip,
So Folks Give Him A Tip,
His Investments Now Hold Quite A Pile There.

A Little Short-Sighted Is Todd,
And He Ordered A Pub Lunch Of Cod,
But The Taste In His Teeth,
Told The Man It Was Beef,
Chef Was Blind, And The Peas Were In Pod.

A Restaurant Waiter Named Trey
Fed A Large Tennis Party Today.
His First Service Was Good,
But He Foot-Faulted The Pud,
And Let New Prawn Balls Go Out Of Play.

A Steam Engine Driver Named Tristan
Was Servicing Motion And Piston,
When A Well-Rounded Bloke
Said, "Are You From The Smoke?"
He Replied, "I'm From Cambridgeshire, Histon."

Travis Doesn't Go Out After Dark,
Though He's Been To Museums And The Park.
But On Cold London Days,
In Bermuda He Stays;
His Seasonal Problem Is Stark.

A Light Aircraft Pilot, Tobias,
Has A Very Strong Home-Town Team Bias.
If His Passengers Choose,
To Wear Reds And Not Blues,
They're Ejected. One Said, "He Won't Fly Us!"

Male U Names

A Conjuring Master Named Ulric
Gave His Helper A Nudge, Or A Small Kick.
Then He Offered Her Money
To Dress Like A Bunny.
She Appeared From His Hat For One Cool Trick.

Ulysses Feels The Breeze Through The Trees,
He's At Ease With His Countryside Wheeze.
But One Time When He Filed
Cross A Field That Was Stiled*,
He Got Stuck And No One Heard His Pleas.

* Had a path through a fence or hedge

A Nice Happy Chappy Ain't Uri,
He's A Ball Of Resentment And Fury.
He Said, "Two Young Goons
Have Just Bent All My Spoons,
And I Hope They're Sent Down By The Jury!"

The Spiraling Debts Of Uzziah
Are Just Getting Higher And Higher.
He Still Works At The Mint,

Where The Bank Notes They Print,
As His Old Money Burns In The Fire!

When Uriah Created A Heap,
It Was Quite Unexpectedly Steep.
He Wanted A Fountain,
But Managed A Mountain,
So He Brought In Some Goats And Some Sheep.

A Crazy Old Chap, Known As Uriel,
Has Always Been Outright Mercurial.
Witty Banter At Pace,
In A Comedy Place,
Though More Measured In The Dock Of A Jury Hall.

Male V Names

When Victor Took Part In The Race,
He Was An Appalling Disgrace.
A Friend Said, "Hey, Vic,
You Have Just Missed A Trick,
And The Slug Beat You Into Twelfth Place!"

Vincent Van's Cough Is Much Worse,
Any Words He Can Say Now, Are Terse.
If He Thinks Juggernaut,
He Becomes Overwrought,
Though He's Still Not Well Versed With A Hearse!

Valentine's Day Of Disaster
Was When He Was Smoothing Some Plaster.
A Blob Fell On His Head,
He Felt A Spring Through His Bed,
And Broke His Watch; Now Time Won't Go Faster!

The Fab And Cool Virgil We Know
Is So Laid Back, And Goes With The Flow.
Does He Think It's The Sixties?
He's Away With The Pixies,
Flower Power, And Let Your Hair Grow!

Little Vernon Is Just Not For Turning,
And He's Had A Remarkable Yearning
To Read People's Minds,
And Extract What He Finds,
To See Why His Ears Keep On Burning!

Vyvyan Sounds A Lot Like A Punk,
But He's Really A Hoarder Of Junk.
He Prefers The Stalls' Patch*
To A "Night At The Match."
If I'd Changed It To "Fight," I'd Be Sunk.

* Area with stalls, or booths

When Vaughn Cut A Field Full Of Corn,
It Took Him From Dusk Until Dawn.
Then He Said, "That's Not Right,
Shouldn't Cut Grain At Night,
The Crop Circles Will Look All Forlorn."

Van The Man Had A Terrible Plan,
But He Thought It Might Work In Japan.
It's A Brand New Quiz Show
Called "Ah, So Tokyo,"
But The Idea Went Straight Down The Pan.

Male W Names

Don't Take William Too Seriously;
He's A Person Of Pure Flippancy.
You May Call Him Silly,
Willie, Will, Bill, Or Billy,
The First And Last Suit Him, Curiously.

When Walter Was Pushing His Trolley*
While Holding Above Him A Brolly*,
The Wind Made Him Take Flight,
To A Dangerous Height;
What A Real Super Man, What A Wally!*

* Trolley: cart; Brolly: umbrella; Wally: silly person

Although Woody Likes Wearing A Hoodie,
He Says, "I'm Not Bad, I'm A Goodie."
He Gets Told In The Shops,
"Hoodie Down, Or The Cops,"
But His Ears Get Quite Cold, So Why Should He?

After Wayne Gained A Sprain Pain In Spain,
He Became So Insane On The Plane,
He Was Locked In A Cage,
For What Seemed Like An Age,
And Was Banned From Their Aircrafts, Again.

Warren Likes All Wild Rabbits And Hares;
When He Spots One, He Stands And He Stares.
Eating Large Lettuce Leaf
With Long Ears And Big Teeth,
Warren Says, "So, I'm Hungry, Who Cares?"

Fashion Guru Wesley Loves Stripes,
And He Helps People Find The Right Types.
But, Unlike On TV,
He Won't Slam You Or Me,
He Is Genuine, Warm, Never Snipes.

A Cautious Home Robber Named Winston
Cleaned The Items He'd Left Fingerprints On,
But The Loot From His Sack
By Mistake He Put Back,
And The Dishes? He Thoroughly Rinsed Them.

A Robotics Expert Named Wilson
All In All Only Has One Grown Real Son.
Though His Household Is Full,
Cyber Families Aren't Cool,
Poor Dress Sense, No Laughs, And No Fun.

When Young Warwick Castled His King,
He Thought It Was Safe On The Wing,
But He Didn't Feel Great,
When He Suffered Checkmate.
He Was Floored, Should He Laugh, Cry, Or Sing?

Wilfred Was Once Left In A Pickle
By Some Colleagues, Who Seemed Rather Fickle.
They Were Old Cold War Spies,
And They Told Him All Lies,
He Was Left With A Hammer And Sickle.

Male X Names

An Image Consultant Named Xander
Told A Colleague He Must Reprimand Her.
So She Answered With Grace,
"You've A Dopey Old Face,
And You Can't Even Charge Me With Slander!"

Got In Far Too Much Trouble, Did Xavier,
Till He Found His One True Savior.
She Became His New Wife,
They're Together For Life,
Though He Has Some Time Off For Good Behavior!

Male Y Names

A Courtroom Affair For Judge Yuri
Saw Decision Split, Causing Him Fury.
And It Sure Got His Goat,
On Just Which Way To Vote,
So He Had To Announce A Hung Jury!

Yehudi Was Wasting Away
At The Start Of His Hospital Stay.
That Was, Up Until
A Good Friend Came To Fill
Yehudi's Menu In, For This Fine Day.

Yusuf Slammed The Front Door,
And The Hinges Are Working No More.
He Didn't Set Out To Break It,
Just Close It, The Poor Twit*,
The Carpet's Too Thin For The Floor.

* Fool

When Yale Went By Rail To The Sale,
There Was Hail, And The Wind Blew A Gale.
The Goodies He Bought

Flew Away, He Had Nought,
He Felt Mugged On A Much Grander Scale.

Yorick's Being Stalked By A Lass.
She's A Schoolgirl, A Pain In The Class.
She Knows Him So Well,
When She Hears The School Bell,
She Follows Him, Hides In The Grass.

A Potential Wine Drinker Is York.
He'd Like Some While Eating His Pork,
But His Bottles Stay Full,
As A Muscle He'd Pull,
If He Tried Removing The Cork.

I Believe That Yves Weaves Prison Sleeves,
And He Smiles While The Governor Seethes.
They're Detachable, See,
So A Grabbed Con Can Flee,
Especially A Jailbird Who Thieves.

A Munitions Worker Named Yitzhak
Needs To Guard Each Explosive On Its Rack.
If An Item Goes West,
There's No Time For A Jest,
He'll Be Faced With A Strong Verbal Blitz-Back.

A Business Executive, Yoram,
Had To Go Into Work, For A Forum.

But On Reaching His Desk,
Saw A Dance Of Burlesque,
It's His Long Service Treat, No Decorum.

Yosef's Dream Boat's Technicolor;
His Old One Was Brown And Much Duller.
But Canal Life Is Hard,
With A Floating Test Card*,
So His Horse Wears Cool Shades, It's The Puller.

* Test Card: TV test pattern

Male Z Names

When Zachary Worked In A Factory,
He Thought He Would Do His Work Tactically.
He Would Not Do A Thing
Unless Bosses Were In,
But They Found Out And Said, "Don't Come Back, See!"

Living With Someone Like Zane,
Is Not All That Good For Your Brain.
With His Eyes Like A Hawk,
And His Strange Double Talk,
He Scares You And Drives You Insane.

A Little Congested Was Zeke,
So Much That He Barely Could Speak.
But He Unblocked His Nose
With A Fireman's Hose,
And Was Mentioned On "Pick Of The Week."

When Zebedee Springs Into Action,
It Usually Gives Satisfaction.
He's A Pogo Stick Tester,
Though He Never Will Pester,
Okay, Then, Perhaps, Just A Fraction.

In A Cycle Contest, Zachariah
Rode Over A Nail Which Wedged Higher.
On Completing The Race,
He Ended Up In Last Place,
Even Though He Got Off To A Flier!

A Very Well-Bred Fed, Named Zed,
Said, "I Dread Being Led To My Bed.
I Do Love My Wife So,
But My Work She Don't Know.
Pillow Talk Kills Careers, Enough Said."

Female A Names

The Bubbly And Artistic Anna
Is Top-Drawer At Creating A Banner.
But The Ones She Don't Like,
She Pins To A Turnpike,
Agitating The Local Town Planner.

Angela Got A Fright From A Tarantula,
On A Small Garden Plant, Right By Her.
She Was Losing Her Cool,
Till The Kids Yelled, "April Fool!"
It Was Rubber, Stringed, Worked By Young Hands, Yeah.

Alexandra Lives In A Large Palace,
Not Buckingham, Crystal, But Dallas.
When She Struts Down The Stairs,
With Her Graces And Airs,
She Has No Aforethought Of Malice.

A Great Movie Turn For Anastasia,
Was Mickey Mouse, When He Starred In "Fantasia."
She Wished She Did Invent This,
The Sorcerer's Apprentice,
The Money Would Make Things Easier For Her!

A Trip To The East For Amanda,
Let Her See, In The Wild, A Panda.
But Her Clodhopper Boots
Crushed Its Fine Bamboo Shoots,
So The Chinese Authorities Banned Her!

An American Artiste Named Amy
Thought The Caterers' Kitchen Too Flamy.
She Said, "Why The Smoke?
Is Your Extractor Broke?"
Said The Chef, "Eat Your Soup, Cockamamie!"

A Dating Agency Failed Alison;
It Was Internet Based, By Comparison.
She Never Met A Man Twice,
Even If He Seemed Nice,
Not Surprising, The Way That She Carried On.

A Well Known Zookeeper Named Andrea
Gets A Glow From Each Newborn She Does Hand-Rear,
So Thank Goodness For Andie,
Whose Bottom Is Sandy,
She Slipped In The Paddock*; Her Legs Are Now Bandier!*

* Paddock: horse pen; Bandier: more bowlegged

When Abigail Took To The Skies,
She Couldn't Believe Her Own Eyes.

When She Looked Through The Glass,
What D'you Think She Saw Pass?
The Good Old Starship Enterprise!

When Alice Was Looking Through Glass,
She Saw The Other Side's Greener Grass.
Is It True What They Say,
That It's Better Their Way?
Or Is That What They Tell You In Class?

A Beautiful Girl Named Alicia
Was Considered A Little Bit Ditzier
Than Her Friends. With Blonde Moments,
She Does Have Her Low Months,
Though Dress-wise She's Classy And Glitzier.

Female B Names

Beatrix Is A Staffordshire Potter,
And Her Kiln Gets So Very Much Hotter,
Than The Arid Death Valley,
Where She Viewed A Car Rally,
The Winner Caked Her With Dust; What A Rotter!*

* Contemptible person

After Barbara Had Brown Windsor Soup,
She Played With Her Blue Hula Hoop.
But She Found It Too Tight
After Snacking All Night,
And Was Pulled Free By Friends In Her Group.

Bernadette Keeps On Getting These Bills,
And It's Making Her Green 'Round The Gills.
She May Just Light A Flame
And Live Up To Her Name,
What She Needs Is A Job And More Skills.

It's Holiday Time For Bianca,
She's Going To Spain's Costa Blanca,
Sun, Sand, And Sangria,

Villas And Paella,
And She Hopes That The Boys Will High-Rank Her.

Bonnie, The Beekeeper's Honey,
Always Makes Big Oodles Of Money.
But When She Paid It In,
The Cashier Threw It In The Bin,
Said, "Nine Buck Notes Are Not Legal, Not Funny!"

Britt Looks Very Fit In Her Kit;
She's A Hit, Full Of Wit, Well, A Bit.
But Her Job Is Not Glamorous,
And You Can't Call It Amorous.
Her Cap Does Stay Lit, Down The Pit.

A Stage Act Performed By Beatrice,
Saw The Audience Boo Her And Then Hiss.
Her Display Was Not Clever,
She Was Under The Weather,
So Today's Matinee She May Miss.

In The Caring Profession Is Brenda;
She Is Known As A Kind Of Befriender.
She'll Discuss All Your Woes,
On A Car Trip, Who Knows,
If Some Money For Fuel You Will Lend Her.

Sky's The Limit For Pretty Belinda,
Providing Her Husband Won't Hinder,
But He Says, "Wait Till Noon
To Go Fly Your Balloon.
At The Moment There's Far Too Much Wind There."

A Telesales Lady Named Belle
Got Nowhere With Her Hard Sell.
So She Tried A Different Ploy,
Now Has No Job, No Joy,
She Ignored Bosses, Who Told Her, "Don't Yell!."

A Six-Foot-Eight Lady Named Bridget
Could Not Be Considered A Midget.
This Basketball Winner,
And Good Finger Ball Spinner,
Relaxes With A Beer Can And Widget.

Female C Names

Charlotte Is A Bit Of A Flirt,
Though She's Sweet Like A Layered Dessert.
If She Gives You The Eye,
Or A Smile That's Wry,
Give One Back, Perhaps More, It Won't Hurt!

Catherine Wheeled* Away In Delight,
After Winning The Big Fight Of The Night.
The Loser Was Horrified
At Being Disqualified,
Though The Ref Had Said Not To Bite.

* A pun on one meaning of Catherine wheel: a torture device

Her Housework Gives Pride To Christine,
So Her Rooms Are Always Pristine.
With A Cloth In Her Hand,
Dust And Cobwebs Are Banned,
Kitchen, Lounge, Bath, And Bedroom Get Swished Clean.

Deejay Caroline's Sweet As A Pear,
On The Air She Seems Honest And Fair.
Oh, But Behind The Scenes,

She Just Plots And She Schemes,
Her Alter Ego Could Give You A Scare.

For The Fancy Dress Party Of Carol,
She Dolled Up In Unusual Apparel,
A Hat Made Of Seaweed,
Licorice Stockings, Indeed,
And Her Dress Was A Large Biscuit Barrel.

After Much-Needed Money Chased Cerys,
In Her Aim To Be A Millionairess.
But Her Last Final Answer
Was Blitzen, Not Prancer,
The Costliest One Of Her Errors.

The Most Fragrant Of Ladies, Named Claire,
Has Just Pinned A Nice Bloom In Her Hair.
It Sure Gives Her Power,
This Lovely Sunflower,
To Catch Radio Waves From The Air.

Cecilia Broke A Man's Heart,
The One With The Rag And Bone Cart*.
He Said, "That's Not Fair,
You Must Pay For Repair,
It Was My Most Dear Work Of Art."

* Rag And Bone Cart: junk peddler'scart

She Was No Oil Painting, Clarissa,
If She Wasn't Here, No One Would Miss Her.
But Now She's In Clover,
With A Massive Makeover,
And She's Found She's A Wonderful Kisser.

The Green-Fingered Townie, Cordelia,
Has A Penchant For Growing Lobelia
The Urban House She Does Rent
Had A Yard Of Cement,
Now It's Green, Far More Touchy And Feelier.

If Cynthia Nicks Someone's Tricks,
Magic Circle's Punishment Sticks,
Though A Wand She Does Crave,
If She Doesn't Behave,
She's The Girl Sawed In Half, What A Fix!.

Female D Names

A Clever Young Lady Named Donna
Copes With Any Crisis Put Upon Her.
She's Sassy, That's True,
Never Turns The Air Blue,
And Was Handed A Wonderful Honor.

On A Trip To The Coast For Davina,
The Golden Beach Couldn't Be Cleaner.
But Although She Had Fun,
She Got Burned By The Sun,
And Her Bright-Red Face Made Her Look Meaner.

Doing Work In The Garden Was Daisy,
Though The Weather Was Just A Tad Hazy.
Then She Called To Her Spouse,
"Hey, I'm Locked Out Of The House!"
Would He Let Her In? No, He's Too Lazy.

Ever Since Her Teen Years, Our Denise
Was Well Known As A Bit Of A Tease.
She Finds If A Man's Ticklish,
While Chewing Her Licorice.
If He's Not, Says Goodbye With Her Knees!

A Celebrity Chef Named Danielle
Was Baking Fantastically Well,
But She Sure Blew Her Top
When The Oven Went "Pop,"
So Now None Of Her Cakes Can She Sell!

Delia's Miffed About What's Going On
In The Sports Hall, Where Something Is Wrong.
When She Plays Table Tennis,
Rotten Eggs Are A Menace,
First There Is A Ping, Then A Pong.

Dorothy Seemed Rather Jolly
On A Walk Down The Street With Her Collie.
She Saw Girls From Her Class,
But Not A Soul Did She Pass,
Without Giggles And Words: "Hello, Dolly!"

She Sure Knows All Her ABCs, Dee,
She's Compiled A Large Dictionary.
But She Got Stuck For Words
When Describing Some Birds,
Said, "They Flap And They Squawk, Can't You See?"

Demi Was Semi-Detached,
But Then Found A Small Cottage That's Thatched.
Now Her Roof Is Quite Bare,

The Last Straw Taken Somewhere,
By A Bird, For A Nest, Eggs Have Hatched!

An I.T. Mishap For Diana
Saw Her Get Herself Stuck In A Scanner.
She Won't Do Things By Half,
Her Office Friends Had A Laugh,
Made Her Body Parts Into A Banner!

A Farm-Working Lady Named Dawn
Rarely Sleeps Past The First Crack Of Morn.
If She Misses The Cockerel,
There's No Cell In Her Clock, Still,
Or Snoring-Proof Ear Muffs She's Worn!

Female E Names

A Witch's Assistant Named Ella
Spent Most of Her Time In The Cellar.
By The Cauldron She'd Stoop,
Stirring Alphabet Soup,
But Got Fired, 'Cause She's Such A Poor Speller!

In Elizabeth's Reign As The Queen
Of Fashion, And New Looks, Unseen,
Trendy Outfits She Wore,
She Paid Not A Dime For,
That Was Up To Her Sponsors, I Mean.

Eleanor Is A Lady Of Leisure,
Her Life Gives Her Financial Pleasure.
"But Why?" You May Ask.
Ellie Once Found A Cask
That Was Chock Full Of Old Pirate Treasure.

A Cheeky* Young Lady Named Eva
Once Pulled A Mechanical Lever,
Made The Clock Change To Ten,

At The Tower Of Big Ben,
Prompting Early Reports By News Reader*.

* Cheeky: brash; reader: news anchor

Young Elaine Took The Strain, Yet Again,
And The Pain To Her Brain Seemed Quite Plain.
So, She Said, "Guys, No More
Anchor Girl, Tug Of War,"
Even Though She Was Built Like A Train!

The College Report For Miss Esther
Involved Badly Wrote Words, Sent To Test Her.
She Was Lying In Bed,
Trying To Read What It Said,
Though She Probably Won't, This Semester.

In A Large Ruined Tower Lived Edwina,
For A Home Switch, She Couldn't Be Keener.
So She Found Herself Lungin'
Into A Large Dungeon,
Not So Light, But So Very Much Cleaner.

The Memory Of Emily's Good, Generally,
With Intelligent Talk, She Acts Venerably.
But She Gave A Blank Look
To A Man, Whose Head Shook,
"I'm Your Ex-Husband," He Said, "Don't You Remember Me?"

A Lover Of Nature, Eugenie,
Doesn't Mind If It's Sunny Or Rainy.
She Just Loves The Outdoors,
Plants, Beaks, Flippers, Or Claws,
She Could Teach You A Lot, She's So Brainy.

Edna's Life Seemed An Average One,
With One Husband, One Daughter, One Son,
Then Her Life Turned One-Eighty,
With Something So Weighty,
A Champagne Lifestyle She Has Won!

Ebony Has An Ivory Tower,
Where She Escapes All Her Stresses, Dear Flower.
Her Bathroom Is Nice,
With A Fragrance Of Spice.
She Oft Soaks There For Over An Hour.

Female F Names

A Cautionary Message From Frances,
While Trying To Teach Ballroom Dances
Was To Let People Know,
It's Slow, Slow, Quick, Quick, Slow.
The Foxtrot's Not A Dance To Take Chances.

A Facsimile Fixer, Fiona,
Didn't Know She'd Just Run Of Toner.
So She Took It Apart,
Put It Back, Wouldn't Start.
Please Don't Fax, You Can Email Or Phone Her.

The Silver Dress Worn By Felicity
Helped Her Enter A Nightclub Illicitly.
Both The Men At The Door
Slipped And Fell To The Floor,
'Cause She Gave Off So Much Electricity!

An Inspector Of Rock Types Is Freya;
She Discovers Things Layer By Layer.
The Ice Age She Knows Most,
And The Jurassic Coast;
She's A Geological Major Player.

In The Diner Where Fay Went Today,
Straight Away With Her Food She Did Play.
But Her Money Was Spent
On A Month Full Of Rent,
So Just How Is She Going To Pay?

The Pain That Was Suffered By Freda
Was Caused By A Fall From A Cedar.
It Tremendously Hurt
When She Fell To The Dirt,
At Least That's What The Rag Tells The Reader.

The Ex-Local-Town-Crier, Fenella,
Now Works As A Door-To-Door Seller.
Council's Choice To Remove Her
Was One Sneaky Maneuver,
Though She Wasn't A Loud Enough Yeller.

A Professional Styling For Florence
Gave Her A Feeling Of Utter Abhorrence.
She Said, "Oh, My Hair
Looks Like Paddington Bear!"
It Improved In The Raindrops, Or Torrents.

A Veteran Cat Burglar, Faith,
Can Unlock Any Combo Of Safe.
But She's Now Rather Old

And Can't Lift Out The Gold;
She's Too Frail, Not A Strong Enough Waif.

It's Usually The High Life For Flavia,
Dines On Champagne And Truffles And Caviar.
She Once Had A Day Off
From Her Life As A Toff*,
Brown Ale, Beans On Toast, We're Not Starving Her!

* A member of the upper classes

She Doesn't Like Too Much Sun, Fern,
Her Skin's Fair, And Will Easily Burn.
One Day In Her Garden,
The Rays Made Her Face Harden.
She Mouthed, "Forecast Said It's Rain's Turn!"

Female G Names

Gloria's Good Wood Was Used
On A Large Ocean Liner That Cruised.
With The Ship Harbor-Bound,
Came A Strong Smell And Loud Sound.
The Wooden Engine Caught Fire, And Fused.

As An Out-And-Out Genius, Gaynor
Is Always An "A" Star Attainer.
Though She Once Got Three Wrong
When Not Fully On Song,
Her Name, Age, And Address, Can You Blame Her?

A Motorbike Rider Named Gillian
Gets Mileage Of Over A Million,
But Still Poor Old Gill,
Hates To Ride Up A Hill,
That's Unless She Is Riding As Pillion!*
Riding As Pillion: Riding in the second seat, behind the driver

Yes, She Fell Down A Well, Gabrielle;
You Could Tell By Her Smell, In The Dell.
But She Rammed In Her Pockets

The Wishing Well's Coin Deposits,
Now Can Buy Anything You Can Sell.

The Enthusiasm Shown By Georgina
Is Not Good, As A Sink And Stove Cleaner,
For The Grill Of Friend's Dad's
Needed Six Brillo Pads,
Any More, Georgie'd Write A Subpoena!

The Damning Indictment Of Gail's
Took The Wind From A Racing Man's Sails.
She Said, "I Am The Judge;
My Position Won't Budge,
You Just Have To Stop Painting Your Snails."

A Hospital Staff Nurse Named Gemma
Gave Her Best, When She Felt An Earth Tremor.
It Was Lunch Time, Of Course,
So She Sealed The Red Sauce.
Real Nosebleeds? Two Fingers. Good Stemmer.

A Young Actress Named Geraldine
Saw Herself As A Star Of The Screen.
Things Went Against Her, You Know,
She Only Made Radio,
She Now Can Be Heard, But Not Seen.

What Gwyneth's Pals Chose For Her Wedding,
For Presents, Just Centered On Bedding.
Though These Gifts Were Not Cheap,
Does She Need All That Sleep?
Each Guest's Wedding List Had The Same Heading.

She Has Style And Elegance, Grace,
Neat And Tidy, No Pin Out Of Place.
But When Past Nine o'clock,
There Is Time For Some Rock,
Lets Her Hair Look A Mess, Playing Bass.

She Is Poor In The Kitchen, That Glenda,
And Once Caught Her Red Hair In The Blender.
So She Now Has A Chef
Who's A Little Bit Deaf.
When He Hears Right, He Cooks Food So Tender.

Female H Names

Ice-Dancing Heather Was Late,
Which Meant Her Skate Partner Must Wait.
She's Been Tardy Now Twice,
And On Very Thin Ice,
But She Makes A Great Figure Of Eight.

A Collector Of British Coins, Hannah,
Has Some Farthings*, Three Ha'pennies*, A Tanner*.
She Keeps Them All In A Tin,
Air Proof; No Rustin',
When They're Worth More She'll Buy Back The Manor!

* Old British coins

A Lawyer Lady Named Hayley
Fell In Love Inside England's Old Bailey*.
To The Beau That She Sought,
She Said, "See You In Court?"
The Judge Said, "Oh, Do You Come Here Daily?"

* Old Bailey: England's Central Criminal Court

A Good Part Of The Team, Now, Is Helen,
And She Certainly Seems To Be Gellin'.

Though It's Tough On Her Back,
As A Girl Lumberjack,
With The Number Of Trees She's Been Fellin'.

Hermione's Stranger Than Fiction,
Though You Must Say She Has Perfect Diction.
But While Eating Her Garlic,
Sounds Like Doctor Who's Dalek*,
A Creator Of Family Friction.

* Dalek(s): Mutated monsters on the "Dr. Who" television show

The Day Of The Week In Which Hazel
Chose To Give All Her Staff Their Appraisal
Was A Monday In June,
From A Hot Air Balloon,
If They Walked Out, They'd Have A Three-Phase Fall.

The Trip Abroad For Henrietta
Saw Her Send Home A Card And A Letter,
Saying, "Wish You Were Here?
I Don't Think So, My Dear."
Now She's Back Home, And Feeling No Better!

A One-Horsepower Woman Is Harriet,
And It Pulls Her Along In Her Chariot.
Although Not Man's Best Friend,
It Can Take A Cool Bend,
If She Were A Mare, She Would Marry It.

A Travel Rep Once Said, "Hi, Heidi"
To A Girl Who Had Just Reached Camp, Friday.
"How D'you Know Me?" She Said,
"Is It Stamped On My Head?"
"Yes, It Is," He Replied, Quite Politely.

Hyacinth Does Have Buckets Of Charm,
Touring Around With A Man On Her Arm.
Though Her Fragrant Bouquet
Has Gone Missing Today,
But, I Don't Want To Sound The Alarm!

A Weather Forecaster Named Holly
Was Always So Bubbly And Jolly.
Last Report, Though, Was Strange,
Satellite Out Of Range,
She Said, "Waterproofs?* Sun Hats? Oh, Golly!"

* Raincoats

Female I Names

When Imogen Left The Armed Forces,
She Undertook Several Courses,
Found Her Specialist Field,
Gave A Lovely Wheat Yield,
Organically Grown, Plowed By Horses!

Isabel Felt Light-Headed And Dizzy
After Slurping From A Can She Thought Fizzy.
But What She Did Demolish,
Was Some Furniture Polish,
Though It Cleansed The Inside Of Poor Izzy.

Iris The Vampirish Diarist
Writes In Blood From A Previously Drier Wrist,
Though It Isn't Her Own,
Just A Limb That's On Loan.
"A Red Letter Day?" Said Her Psychiatrist.

A Star Of The Screen, Named Irene,
Likes The Softness Of Polystyrene.
Does This Mean She's Protected?
No More Than Expected,
She Packs Plasmas, Know What I Mean?

An Electronics Girl, Isolde,
Knows How To Apply Perfect Solder.
Printed Circuits Are Fine,
Never Crossing The Line,
Capacity For Resistance She'd Shoulder.

A Sprint-Jumping Athlete Was Isla,
Whose Hurdles Were Almost As High As Her.
When She Crashed In Mid-Race,
She Then Said, To Save Face,
"I Believe I Am More Of A Miler."

Quite A Novice To Dancing Was Ivy,
But She Said, "Oh, How Hard Can The Jive Be?"
Then She Hit The Dance Floor,
Found Her Timing Was Poor,
And Blamed The Music For Being Too Lively.

A Young Mezzo-Soprano Named Ingrid,
As A Child, Won The Crown Of Best Sing Kid.
Some Glass Trophies She Won,
Sadly, Now She Has None;
They Got Smashed By Her Voice, Everything Did!

A Big Animal Lover, Ione,
Enjoys Jumping With Her Little Pony.
Just Small Fences, With Stiles*,

Ponies From Shetland Isles,
She Has Two, So They Will Not Get Lonely.

* Steps for climbing over a wall or fence

A Clumsy Young Lady Named India
Got Caught Out, When The Weather Got Windier.
She Fell From A Tree,
Badly Grazed Her Right Knee.
But It's Not Her Strong Leg, So It Won't Hinder Her!

The Flyaway Hairdo Of Irma
Meant She Asked Her Hairdresser To Perm Her.
Her Locks Became Plump,
From A Bicycle Pump,
Yes It's Quite Solid Now, And Much Firmer!

Female J Names

As Stiff As A Board Now, Is Jacqueline,
After Doing Veneer Work And Lacquerin'.
To Her Husband, Said Jackie,
"Hey, I'm Not Your Lackey,
Now, Do The Wallpaper, And Carpet Tackin'."

With Jane On A Slow Train In Spain,
She Became Quite Insane In The Brain.
Heading Down To The South,
Seville Tongue Not In Mouth,
She Turned Orange In The Face, Yet Again.

Joan Won't Take A Loan On The Phone,
As No Car And No Home Does She Own.
All Cold Callers Get Miffed
When She Gives Them Short Shrift,
As She Very Much Dislikes Their Tone!

Full Of Punch Now Is Judith, Or Judy,
And Maybe The Upside Of Moody.
After Many A Slurp,
There Was More Than One Burp,
Potent Drink Left Her Fruity And Broody.

A Laboratory Worker Named Julia
Thinks She May Have Just Cloned Number Two Of Her.
The Big Test Tube Mistake,
Spawned A Phony, Or Fake,
Though The Bolt In Her Neck Is Peculiar.

The Round Of Hot Drinks Bought By Jill
Left Her Waiting An Hour To Fill,
And She Nearly Had Pups,
Holding Ninety-Six Cups,
Though Not One Single Drop Did She Spill!

Dancing Queen Josephine Looked So Lean,
She Was Keen On The Discotheque Scene.
Now, After Her Levities,
It's Gone Nineteen-Seventies,
But She Still Can't Be Called A Has-Been.

A Practical Girl Named Joanna
Plumbed Away, In A Cordial Manner,
Employed By The White House,
To Clear Pipes With Her Nous,
And Was Given A Star Spangled Spanner!

A Primary Teacher Named Julie
Can Combat Any Child Who's Unruly,
Not With Stick, Or With Carrot,

But Her High-I.Q. Parrot,
Teaching Children A Lesson, Yes, Truly!

A Prototype Test Driver, Jean,
Rides A Buggy, Cart, Or Dream Machine.
One Had A Top Speed Of Five,
And Was Barely Alive,
An Unpimped Ride, That's Smelly, Unclean!

A Struggling College Girl, Jade,
Feared She Wouldn't Be Making The Grade.
Then She Turned On Her Brain,
Got To Grips With The Strain,
Now A World Leader, She's Glad That She Stayed!

Female K Names

A Triathlon Competitor, Kirsty,
Drank Loads In The Heat, She Was Thirsty.
When Swim And Cycle Did End,
She Had A Lead To Defend,
But She Ran In Plum Last, Late On Thursday!

Kylie's Big Gnome Had A Friend,
And They Fished In The Pond Till The End.
But The Friend Lost His Beard,
It Was Totally Sheared,
And The Vandal Was Clean 'Round The Bend.

Escape Artist Kate Is Just Great;
She Gets Out Just In Time, Never Late.
And I'll Tell You This, Matey,
Strong Ties, Has Young Katie,
And Can Unrope A Figure Of Eight.

Karen's New Carpentry Skills
Are Helping To Pay Household Bills.
Chairs And Tables Of Teak,
Will One Day Be Antique,
Though They're Already Ringing The Tills.

Keira's Nightly Ambition Was Wishing
To Take A Rod And Go Midnight Fishing.
But Just What Made Her Bark?
Not Afraid Of The Dark,
Just The Teeth Of The Pike She Was Kissing.

So Clean Out Of Gossip Was Kayleigh,
Not Good News When You Work For A Daily.
A Blank Space For Her Column,
Editor Looking Solemn,
Then She Said, "A Scoop's On Its Way, Maybe."

After Katherine Squealed With Delight
When She Met A Guy, Bonfire Night,
She Said, "Here For A Reason?"
He Said, "Gunpowder*, Treason."
She Replied, "Well, It's Love At First Sight!"

* Gunpowder: a reference to the Gunpowder Plot of 1605 to
  assassinate King James I

A Day In Court, Forced On Kristina,
By A Legally Binding Subpoena,
Left The Judge With Scratched Head,
When Her Twin Came Instead.
He's A Man And Said, "Nobody's Seen Her."

An Industrious Lady Named Kara
Drilled For Oil In The Southern Sahara.
But The Sand Was Wrong Type,
And It Clogged Up Her Pipe,
Plus, There Wasn't An Alcohol Bar There.

Krystal Is Clear About Something;
She Delights In A Bit Of Tub-Thumping*,
Her Words Hurt Like A Sting,
With A Dominant Ring,
Into Her You Would Hate To Be Bumping.

* Arguing or promoting something vigorously

A Cycling Novice Named Keeley
Was Surprised She Could Manage A Wheelie.
When Her Front Left The Turf
For The First Time Since Birth,
The Two Back Wheels Saved Her, No, Really.

Female L Names

Lorraine Chased Some Kids Down The Lane,
Nuisance Calls Caused Her Terrible Strain.
But She's Now A Lot Trimmer
And Has Foregone The Zimmer*,
Her Mobility's Perfect, Again.

* Any product from Zimmer, a manufacturer of orthopedic products

On A Milestone Birthday For Lisa,
Her Partner Tried So Hard To Please Her.
When The Party He Planned
Just Got So Out Of Hand,
She Asked Police, "Breach Of The Peace, Sir?"

She Gives Off An Aura, Does Laura.
Something Richer? At Least It's Not Poorer.
She Glides Round Her Place
With A Bright, Sparkly Face,
Though Her Servants Now Mostly Ignore Her.

"The Fate That Befell Poor Louise,
Is A Thing That Has Caused Me Unease,"

Were The Words Of A Man
In A Small Ice Cream Van,
Rocket Popsicles Gave Her Brain Freeze.

Lesley's A Girl For Each Season,
And She Certainly Has A Good Reason.
Spring Flowers She Picks,
Summer Ice Cream She Licks,
Fall Harvest, And Skis When It's Freezing!

A Haphazard Climber Named Lily
Picks Herself Up Quite Often, When Hilly.
Sometimes Crawls Like The Spider
That's Sat Down Beside Her,
But With Two Legs, Not Eight, Don't Be Silly!

An Expert Race Driver, Lucille,
Lost A Hubcap While Speeding Uphill,
Flung The Door, With A Clang,
Then She Got Out And Sang,
"You Picked A Fine Time To Leave Me, Loose Wheel!"

Water Buckets Were Drawn By Letitia,
From A Walled Hole Full Of Water, No Fish There.
She Leaned Over Too Far,
Fell Down, Got A Scar,
And Was Hit By A Coin From A Well Wisher!

The Chariot Race Plan Of Leanne
Didn't Quite Go According To Plan.
Almost Straight From The Start,
She Lost Control Of Her Cart,
So She Ran And She Ran And She Ran!

A Daredevil Stuntwoman, Leah,
Is No Stranger To Danger, Or Fear.
There Are Down Sides And Pluses,
When You Jump Nineteen Buses.
When Successful, She Orders A Beer!

On A Camping Excursion, Our Linda,
Tried Lighting A Fire With Tinder,
Staying Up Half The Night,
Trying To Set Twigs Alight,
Did Her Partner Help? No, He Did Hinder!

Female M Names

The Extreme Sports Participant, Mary,
Will Try Anything Once, If It's Scary.
With Each Cut, Scrape, And Bruise,
It's A Brave Life To Choose,
Though The Scale Of Each Problem May Vary.

Michaela's Tracking Adventure Went Well,
And She's Many A Tale Now To Tell.
When She Saw A Wild Boar,
She Lay Downwind, On The Floor,
So It Couldn't Pick Up Her Scent/Smell.

Maureen's Lip Manages Motion,
Like A Fifty-Foot Wave In The Ocean.
She Can Talk Till She Drops,
When The Ozone Layer Pops,
Or Can No Longer Think Of A Notion.

An Equestrian Rider Named Madeleine
Hit A Fault With The Horse She's Been Straddlin',
Got Tipped Off At A Jump,
Fell To Earth With A Bump,
Through The Water Now, She Is Still Paddlin'.

A Comedy Rogue Named Melissa
Was Named Hollywood's Stupidest Kisser.
A Co-Star Once Froze,
After A Peck On The Nose,
And An Eyebrow/Ear Slurp For Well-Wisher.

A Medical Student, Maxine,
Developed A New Kind Of Vaccine,
Using Mashed Up Papyrus;
It Kills Every Virus,
And Is Made Into Pills, By Machine.

A Broad-Shouldered Girl Named Matilda
Works On Site, As An Office Block Builder.
With The Bricks That She Stacks,
There's No Way You'll See Cracks,
Belly Laughs With The Boys Nearly Killed Her!

A Young Fairytale Princess Named Marilyn
Reverse-Kissed The Prince She Was Marryin'.
Something Jumped From A Log,
Her Betrothed, Kermit Frog,
Him Straight Over The Threshold She's Carryin'!'

A Magician's Assistant, Martina,
Was, Compared To Her Master, Much Keener.
When He Sawed Her In Half,

He Did Yawn, She Did Laugh;
Since The Vanishing Act, No-One's Seen Her!

A Well-To-Do Girl Named Michelle
Likes Pretending She's Not Very Well.
Nurse Helped Her To The Lavatory,
She's Been Fooling Her, Hasn't She,
Pull The Chain, And Stop Ringing Your Bell!

A Fright In The Night, For Madonna,
Made Her Think She Was Almost A Goner.
The Material She Wears
Didn't Come Down In Pairs,
The Whole Wardrobe Had Fallen Upon Her!

Female N Names

A Young Party Girl Named Naomi
Turned Bright Green, Her Mouth Was All Foamy.
It's Her Time Of The Month,
To Drink Neat Crème De Menthe,
Or Mouthwash. Are Her Teeth Clean? Please Show Me.

Nanette's Pet Dog Met The New Vet,
Before Licking The Poor Man's Face Wet.
Then He Said, "There's No Charge,
Your Hound's Not Very Large,
All She Needs Is A Shampoo And Set!"

The Normally Svelte-Looking Nadia
Was Becoming A Little Bit Lardier,
Till Her Push-Up Regime
Got Her Back In The Team,
Now, She's Fitter, And Fresher, And Hardier.

Nancy Works At The Local Casino;
Such A Lot Of Hard Cash She Has Seen Go.
When She Has Enough Bread,
It's Las Vegas To Wed,
Before An Obvious Trip Down To Reno.

A Stern Sort Of Woman Is Nicola,
For The Rules She Is Always A Stickler.
But She Does Have One Weakness,
And I Will Not Repeat This,
She Barks Every Time That You Tickle Her!

A True Free-Range Farmer Is Natalie,
She Brings Chickens Home From The Battery,
And Her Milk Is So Pure,
That You'll Love It For Sure,
Not From Hens, But From Cows, Yes, The Latterly.

An Intelligent Lady Named Nina
Is The Internet Highway's Top Gleaner.
Though She Knows All That Stuff,
It Is Never Enough,
There Is Always A Pasture That's Greener.

No, You Shouldn't Be Messing With Nyree.
Her Blood Boils So Fast, She Is Fiery.
If You Get In A Quarrel,
Scratch Your Head, Like Stan Laurel,
And Then Write Caustic Thoughts In Your Diary.

A Cheerleading Lady Named Norma
On A Hot Day Was Getting Much Warmer.
Her Tassels Caught Fire,

And The Routine Was Quite Dire,
And The Gridiron Wasn't A Stormer.

She Turns Up Uninvited, Natasha,
As A Wedding-, Birth-, Funeral-Crasher.
If You Don't Apprehend Her,
She'll Go On To Attend A
Bar Mitzvah, Divorce, Baby-Splasher.

Office Work Is Quite Humdrum For Niamh,
Leaves Her Head Spinning, Would You Believe?
Typing, Faxing, And Phone,
Boss And Colleagues Who Drone,
Perhaps One Day She'll Get A Reprieve.

Female O Names

The Mansion That Houses Olivia,
With A Woodland And Beautiful River Near,
Is Somewhat In Decay;
To The Bailiffs She'd Say,
"I'm A Squatter; Illegally Living Here!"

A Girl From East Europe Named Olga
Was Rushing Off, Clasping A Folder.
She Will Go Home Today,
If The Law Has Its Way;
She's A Spy, And The Document's Vulgar.

An Upstanding Lady Is Orla;
Of The People She Knows, She's Much Taller.
With Her Head In The Clouds,
As She's Walking Through Crowds,
She Takes A Moment To Hear, When You Call Her.

When Oprah Opened Canned Fruit,
She Spilled A Bit Of It Down A Friend's Suit,
Then She Let Out A Scream
Over Peaches And Cream,
Cut Her Thumb On The Can, Not So Cute.

When Ophelia Went To The Opera,
She Was Seated Way Up At The Top There,
With Her Glasses And Flask,
And An Oxygen Mask,
She Said, "Why Do We Find This So Popular?"

Olive's Oil Reserves Are Now Low,
And She's Letting Refineries Know.
Didn't Want To Sound Rude,
But A Tap Full Of Crude
Makes The Dishes Black; Water Should Flow!

Opal Is A Pure PC Beauty,
And She Won't Accept Language That's Fruity.
Super Svelte, But So Tough,
Her Job Is Quite Rough,
Police Person? She Sure Does Her Duty.

Her Choice Meal Style Is Indian,*Ocean,
So Hot, That Her Mouth Was Just Roastin',
So, She Went Straight Back Home,
With Jaw Starting To Foam,
She Soothed It With Remedy Lotion.

* Indian = Indian meal, for example, curry.

A Big Fan Of Lawn Tennis, Odette,
Likes To Try An Occasional Win Bet.

Wagering The In Play,

Thought The Next Point Would Pay,

But The Other Girl Won, Game And Set.

Top Salon Hairdresser, Octavia,

Likes To Make Clients' Styles Much Wavier.

She Refers To A Book

For The Ladies' New Look,

Better Cuts Than In London's Belgravia*

* A very wealthy area of London

An Old-Fashioned Girl, Oriana,

Is A Cook, Cleaner, Washer, And Darner.

But She Does Tell Tall Tales

From Her Childhood In Wales.

Slain A Dragon? She Is Such A Nana!**

* A woman who cares for others' children
* Nana – Sounds like two-thirds of a banana – British slang for a
   fool

Female P Names

A Digital TV Girl, Paula,
Got A Job As A Cable Installer.
Frequencies She Did Find,
Tested Pause And Rewind,
Better Than Her Last Post, Bingo Caller!

When Her Duty Tour Started, Patricia
Got A Send-off From Every Well-Wisher.
But Pat's Gun Fired Blanks,
So She Dropped Down The Ranks,
And Could Not Even Make The Militia.

Philippa Cooks Cottage Pie,
Mashed Potatoes, Meat, Onions, No Lie!
Pippa Does Like Her Carrots,
They're Not All For The Parrots;
"My Food's Healthy!" She Says, By The By.

A Partnership Phobia Had Phoebe
For Her Husband, Who Dressed Like A Bee Gee.
She Thought He Would Leave Her,
With Saturday Night Fever,
But He Was Still There On Sunday, He Need Be.

When Petula Clocked In Before Work,
She Dreamt Of Receiving Her Perk,
Thought She'd Been There Ten Years,
Drenched The Floor With Her Tears,
She'd Miscounted, It Was Nine, Went Berserk!

A Bored Office Worker Named Poppy
Has A Laugh When The Printer Won't Copy.
When Computers Do Jam,
She Dismantles The RAM,
And Says, "Yes, I Am Feeling Quite Floppy."

A Window Box Given To Pandora
Had Spectacular, Colorful Flora.
But Her Children Did Play,
Couldn't Keep Balls Away,
Plants Got Crumpled, Not What We'd Planned For Her.

She's A Bit Of A Tomboy, Is Paige,
But Her Parents Say, "That's Just A Stage."
Though She Likes Rough Sports, Jeans,
And Dirty Hands On Machines,
She'll Grow Into Her Dresses, With Age.

A Fine Motown Dancer Is Pamela,
Knowing All The Right Moves To Do Tamla*.
Though Her Voice Is A Fright,
She Can Mime, Bop, All Night,

As She Has Unbelievable Stamina.

* Original name of the Soul Music label, Motown Records

Penelope Took A Pit Stop En Route,
Before Her Recital On Flute.
But In Her Mad Chase
From Rest Room, Grabbed Wrong Case,
Penny Whistle, Though—Sounded Quite Cute.

An Arctic Explorer Named Pearl
Thought She'd Give The North Pole One More Whirl.
Trudging Through Snow And Ice,
The Weather Wasn't Very Nice,
And Her Flag Froze, And Wouldn't Unfurl!

Female Q Names

Aladdin Was Once Watched By Queenie;
Her Favorite Part Was The Lamp And The Genie.
The Three Wishes She'd Choose:
A New Car, And New Shoes,
And A Spanking-New Summer Bikini.

When Queen Set Off Her Catherine Wheel*,
It Made An Unusual Squeal.
Though It's Now The New Year,
All The Sounds That We Hear,
Are Not Happy; She Bought A Raw Deal.

* Catherine wheel: a rotating firework that produces sparks and
   colored flames

Female R Names

Rachel Went For Her Diamonds And Pearls,
To Wear On A Night Out With The Girls,
But A Thief Had Picked Locks
On Each Jewelry Box,
Stole The Lot, Even Gifts From The Earls.

She Really Is Clumsy, Rebecca,
And She Tripped Up Bus Stairs, Double-Decker.
Then She Soared To The Top,
Hit The Bell, Request Stop,
Accidently; Got Off, Then Home Trekker.

She's Not All That Tall, Is Roxanne,
But She Longs To Be Big In Japan.
She's The Rock And Roll Queen,
Star Of Stage And Of Screen,
At Least, That's Her Big Master Plan.

A Top Toupee Seller, Renee,
Is Doing Great Business Today.
Every Style Has She Managed
For The Follicular Challenged;
Even Folk From The Courtroom Will Pay.

Rosemary Has A Very Short Time
To Write A Fun, Suitable Rhyme
For The Local Newsletter.
Rosie's Wanting To Better
Last Month's Winner; Now Is That A Crime?

Quite Pleasant In Nature Is Ruth,
But Sometimes She Appears Quite Aloof.
When Her Wardrobe's A Mess,
Demon Eyes Look Ruthless,
Not A Girl For The Mornings, In Truth.

A Junior Office Temp, Rhona,
Filled The Copier Up With Some Toner.
She Thought Black Ink Wouldn't Harden,
So She Filled It With Tartan*.
Now, Her Agency Will Never Phone Her.

* A brand of ink sold in Britain

As A Top Catwalk Model, Roberta
Is Considered A Bit Of A Flirter.
On One Runway Walkthrough,
She Winked Her Eye At A Few,
But It Didn't Completely Exert Her!

As A Drainage Assistant, Rhianna
Is Well Used To A Pipe And A Spanner*.

But She Hopes By The Summer,
She'll Be The Number One Plumber,
And Receive Her Commemorative Banner.

* A wrench

On A Freezing Cold Winter's Day, Rita
Decided To Crank Up The Heater.
With Her Clothing Of Wool,
She Is Warmed To The Full;
You Could Call Her A Real Toasty Bleater!

A White Witch From Wales, Raquel,
Is Quite Thorough When Casting A Spell.
"Only Good Ones, Of Course,"
She Says, Mixing Her Sauce,
What She Needs Them For, No One Can Tell.

Female S Names

A Fashion Guru Named Sarah
Is Always The Slickest Clothes-Wearer.
Even Threads That She Wore,
From A Second Hand Store,
She Pimped Up, Oh, Just What Could Be Fairer?

At The Fancy Dress Ball, Young Samantha
Dressed Up As A Black-Colored Panther.
This Cat Caused Guests Fear,
They Could Hear, But Not See Her,
Lights Were Out, But They Could Smell The Camphor.

Several Quality Names Rhyme With Sharon,
But I'm Leaving This Rhyme Slightly Barren.
You Can Think For Yourself,
Because Knowledge Is Wealth,
But For Lady Luck, Marry A Baron.

Beauty Products, As Tested By Susan,
You Could Say, Were Not Quite Of Her Choosin'.
But Her Dash For The Cash,
Gave Her Quite A Bad Rash;
Allergies Are Not Quite So Amusing.

A Receptionist Girl Named Selina
Also Works Part-Time As A Store Cleaner.
So She Earns Extra Cash,
And She Cuts A Fair Dash,
Phone To Floor And Then Home, She Is Keener.

Stephanie Is Mad Keen On The Garden,
But She's Quite Hard Of Hearing, Though—Pardon?
To Hear Whispering Grass
She May Need A Bypass,
Though Perhaps It's Ear Wax That Did Harden.

A Daring Peak Climber Named Sylvia
Thinks Of Every New Challenge As Hill V* Her.
She Cut Short One Go,
Mouthing "Darn," "Dash," And "Blow,"
But She Swore That The Weather Was Filthier!

* Versus

A Naval Lieutenant Named Sandra
Takes Her Duty List From Her Commander.
She Hates His Tone Of Voice,
But Does Not Have A Choice,
Though She Once Thought She'd Sue Him For Slander.

On A Quick Getaway, Our Sienna
Shot Off To The City, Vienna.

Sights Were Great, As Suggested,

But She Did Get Arrested,

Falsely So, But Bribed Guards With Some Henna.

A Fruitarian, Well Known As Sherrie,

Got Her Ear Blocked Up With A Stray Berry.

Then Her Doctor Said, Flat,

"I Have Some Cream For That.

Pour It In Twice A Day, You'll Feel Merry."

Female T Names

An Athlete Of Note, Name Of Tina,
Runs Cross Country, She's Leaner And Meaner.
As She Dashed Round One Course,
With Incredible Force,
She Was So Fast, Nobody Could See Her.

A Lingerie Model Named Tracy
Went To Wear Something Frilly And Lacy.
But Around Two o'clock
Gave The People A Shock,
As The Outfit She Wore Was So Racy.

A Demanding Boss, Known As Teresa,
Has A Staff That Will Try To Appease Her.
They Will Grovel Like Mad,
To Keep Their Jobs Safe; It's Sad,
That's Unless They're A Good Looking Geezer!

A Junior Professor Named Tessa
Confesses To Being A Guesser
Of The Big Bang Theories,
And The Root Of All Trees,
But, She's Just Early Teens; I Say, "Bless Her."

A Plump-Looking Lady Named Trudy
Was Considered A Bit Of A Foodie.
But She Doesn't Eat Much;
Yes, She Has Curves, As Such,
But She's Pregnant, Or Big-Boned And Broody.

A Princess Of Beauty, Named Tara,
Was Wearing A Sparkling Tiara.
On A Big Night Of Glamour,
Where The Cameramen Clamor,
The Next Bingo Commercial Will Star Her.

A Chemistry Expert Named Tabitha
Likes Her Old Feline Pet In The Lab With Her.
Tabby's Cat Won't Sit Still,
And Laps Up Every Spill;
It's The Only Green Persian With Rabbit Fur!

Quite Prolific Is Screen Queen Tamara;
You Can't Miss Seeing Something That Stars Her.
At A Big Awards Spiel,
The Host Said, "Are Those Teeth Real?"
So She Bit Him And Said, "Yes, They Are, Sir!"

On A Zoo Trip, A Young Girl Named Tanya
Fell In Love With A Good Looking Panda.
She Soon Whipped It Away,

Brought It Back The Next Day,
It's A Brit Police Car; They Did Ban Her.

A Slow-Minded Lady Named Tiffany
Has Just Suddenly Had An Epiphany.
From Her Life On The Dole*,
She Now Sings Rock & Roll,
And Remembers The Song Lyrics Spiffingly*.

* Dole: welfare; Spiffingly: excellently

Female U Names

A Music Technician Named Una
Is The World's Finest Piano Tuner.
She Makes Mozart And Bach
Seem A Walk In The Park,
A Little Night Music's So Lunar.

The Trouble With Ursula's Curse
Is, It's Not Getting Better, But Worse.
She Was Struck With A Hex,
By A Witch She Did Vex,
And, Right Now, She's In Need Of A Nurse.

A Mild Law Breaker Is Unity,
And The Courts Treated Her With Impunity.
The Judge Said, "I Don't Think
You Should Be In The Clink.
Jaywalkers Stay In The Community."

Female V Names

When Victoria Falls Off A Horse,
Does She Get Right Back On? Yes, Of Course.
Nothing's Ever Too Tricky
For A Lady Like Vicky.
She Has Stamina, Strength, Straight From Source.

During A Critique By Valerie
At The Local Municipal Gallery,
She Rendered Scant Praise
To What Looked Like A Graze,
But, It's Worth An Extremely Large Dowry!

That Overstretched Lady, Vanessa,
Works Her Days As A Push-Button Presser.
With A Family To Feed,
And A Garden To Weed,
Any More And It Really Would Stress Her!

A Lover Of Cats Is Virginia,
With Her Breed That Comes From Abyssinia,
With Their Brown And Black Fur,
Fairly Short, As They Purr,
She Empties The Litter Tray, Ginny, Yeah..

The First Rocket Fired By Vivienne
Barely Took Off, Too Much Of A Heavy One.
The Next One Was Lighter,
She Got Inside It To Flight Her,
Saying, "Now It's The Moon, Or Oblivion!"

The One-Woman Band, Named Veronica,
Plays The Drums, Cymbals, Whistle, Harmonica.
But With All Of Her Curves,
Ronnie Regularly Swerves,
And Sometimes She Hits Her Japonica*.

* A shrub with glossy green leaves and aromatic flowers

On A Stormy Sea Crossing, Our Velma
Enquired, "Who Is That At The Helm, Sir?"
She Was Told "It's On Auto,"
As They Sailed To Oporto.
Although Shocked, It Did Not Overwhelm Her.

On A Viennese Venture, Our Vera
Asked If They Still Would Take Lira.
Then She Said, "No, That's Venice,
A Terrible Menace,
And I Reckon The Whirls Here Are Dearer."

Venus Does Have A Brain Like A Planet,
And The Toughness Of Aberdeen Granite.

Her Twinkling Eyes, She Does Roll,
Quite Unlike A Black Hole,
Shooting Star? I Would Bottle, Or Can It.

A Wall Decorator Named Violet
Was Struggling To Make A Small Tile Fit.
Her Boss Got Annoyed
As Vi Fumbled And Toyed,
Then She Told Him She Might Have To File It.

Female W Names

She's Up With The Times, Is Young Wendy,
Hair And Clothes Are So Terribly Trendy.
But Although It's Her Passion,
It Costs Money, This Fashion,
So She Recycles Things Shiny And Bendy.

Absence, For Poor Dear Old Wanda,
Never Did Make Her Heart Grow Much Fonder.
The Sailor She Did Court
Had A Girl In Each Port.
She Found Out, As He Toured The Blue Yonder.

On A Sporting Day Out, Wilhelmina
Entered Into A Giant Arena.
It Was Way Out In Philly,
The Wrong Place, Silly Billie,
She Saw Baseball, Not Basketball, Played There.

She's Got Plenty Of Friends, Does Winona,
Though She Still Feels A Bit Of A Loner.
Since Her Voice Is Not Loud,
It Gets Lost In The Crowd.
If You Hear No Reply, Maybe Phone Her?

I Think Whitney May Just Love This,
It's The One Thing She Won't Want To Miss.
Is It Birthdays Or Weddings?
No, A Sale On Some Beddings,
Nighty Night, Bed Bugs Bite, And A Kiss.

When Wilma Was Mopping The Floor,
She Slipped And Became Very Sore.
When She Got Back On Her Feet,
She Was White As A Sheet,
And Would Sue Herself, If She Had More.

A Tiny Young Lady Named Winifred
Likes To Do All Her Chores In A Pinny*, Red.
She's A House-Proud Home-Stayer,
Partner's Basketball Player,
The Pair Have A King-Size, And A Mini Bed.

* A sleeveless jumper

There Was Far Too Much Wind Speed For Willow,
As Her Camping Tent Started To Billow.
The Breeze Ran Out Of Puff,
But Did Damage Enough,
And I'm Sure There Were Tears On Her Pillow.

Female X Names

Xanthe's Favorite Shade Is Pale Yellow,
And This Wall Color Makes Her Feel Mellow.
One That's Blue- Or Green-Hued
Will Not Upset Her Mood,
But A Blood-Red One Might Make Her Bellow.

The Exotically Named Xaviera
Took A Trip To The French Riviera.
She Then Fell Off Her Yacht,
Bounced, And Found A Nice Spot,
Then Breathed All The Lovely Sea Air There.

Our Xena's A Worrying Type,
And She Never Eats Fruit That's Not Ripe.
Cautious She May Be,
But, Sensible, Baby,
If You Choose To Believe All The Hype.

The Favorite Cult Film Seen By Xenia
Is The Rockers' And Mods'* *Quadrophenia.**
The Main Thing She Likes
Is The Size Of Their Bikes;

Younger Actors Have Now Become Senior.

* Mods: rebellious British teenagers in the sixties; Quadrophenia: A
  film about a boy and his scooter-riding friends

Female Y Names

A Spend, Spend, Spend Girl, Yvonne,
Needed Cash For Her Spree To Go On.
But Her Finance Scheme Sank
When She Raided A Bank;
It Was Closed, And The Money Was Gone.

A Trumpet Musician Named Yasmin
Is At Home When Displaying Her Jazz Thing.
She Also Plays The Trombone,
Clarinet, And Saxophone,
So She Certainly Isn't A Has-Been.

At An Animal Shelter, Yvette
Wanted So To Take Home A New Pet,
Not A Cat, Or A Dog,
But A Bat, Or A Frog,
She Doesn't Mind The Dark, Or The Wet.

A Top Golfer On Her Home Course, Yolanda,
Drove Lots Of Balls Into The Ground There.
Her Aim Was Usually True,
Often Putting From Two;
She Had The Wrong Clubs For A Left-Hander.

She's So Into Fitness, Yelena,
And Has Hired A Personal Trainer,
Who Does Drive Her Hard,
To Remove All The Lard,
But He's Careful And Doesn't Over-Strain Her.

"Oh, No!" Said Unfortunate Yoko,
As She Rowed Down The River Orinoco.
Her Control Was So Poor
That Her Boat Lost An Oar;
She Will Not Be In Time For Her Cocoa!

Female Z Names

Zoe Seemed Like A Wonderful Daughter,
Doing All The Things Father Had Taught Her,
Until, One Day She Changed,
And Her Life Rearranged,
Punished Crime Meant She Got Bread And Water.

A Medical Doctor Named Zara
Was In Italy, Namely, La Scala.
But While Watching The Opera,
She Became Very Popular,
Pried A Man From His Glasses, No Scar There.

English Cross-Channel-Swim-Race-Girl, Zena,
Had No Goose Fat, So She Used Margarine There.
Her Heart Was A-Flutter,
But No Worse Than Butter;
When She Won, She Did Feel A Lot Cleaner.

A Working Apprentice Named Zelda
Was Training To Be A Spot Welder.
Before Working With Metal,
She Got Used To The Kettle.
"Your Brew Is Just Fine," Said An Elder.

A Secondary Teacher Named Zeta
Has A Technique That's Very Much Neater
For Writing On Blackboards
With Clean-Looking White Words;
She Warms Up The Chalk On The Heater.

International Cricketer Zola,
Is Known As A Very Fast Bowler.
Leg Before*, Stumped*, Catch Hero,
Or Bowled Out For Zero*,
Before Time For A Rest And A Cola.

* Leg before (wicket), stump: references to throwing the batter out;
  Bowled out for a zero: kept the other side from scoring any runs